Social Literacy

Social Literacy

A Social Skills Seminar
for Young Adults with
ASDs, NLDs, and Social Anxiety

by

Mary Riggs Cohen, Ph.D.
Asperger Center for Education and Training
New York

·PAUL·H·
BROOKES
PUBLISHING Cº.®

Baltimore • London • Sydney

Paul H. Brookes Publishing Co.
Post Office Box 10624
Baltimore, Maryland 21285-0624
USA

www.brookespublishing.com

Typeset by Integrated Publishing Solutions, Grand Rapids, Michigan.
Manufactured in the United States of America by
Versa Press, Inc., East Peoria, Illinois.

The images used in the slide presentations on the accompanying CD-ROM
copyright © 2011 Jupiterimages Corporation.

Case examples are based on the author's experiences. Names and identifying details have been
masked to protect confidentiality.

Library of Congress Cataloging-in-Publication Data

Cohen, Mary Riggs.
    Social literacy : a social skills seminar for young adults with ASDs, NLDs, and social anxiety /
by Mary Riggs Cohen.
        p.   cm.
    Includes bibliographical references and index.
    ISBN-13: 978-1-59857-068-7 (pbk.)
    ISBN-10: 1-59857-068-4 (pbk.)
    1. Youth with mental disabilities—Life skills guides.   2. Learning disabled youth—Life skills
guides.   3. Social skills—Study and teaching.   I. Title.
HV1568.3.C64 2011
646.7'60874—dc22   2010053953

British Library Cataloguing in Publication data are available from the British Library.

2015   2014   2013   2012   2011

10   9   8   7   6   5   4   3   2   1

Contents

Contents of the Accompanying CD-ROM

Note: The training and class presentation materials are on this CD-ROM in separate slide files; click on the applicable link to open the desired slide file. There are no slides for Class 6 (Outing with Social Coaches) or Class 12 (Final Class Party). See the Handouts folder on this CD-ROM for the individual handout files; refer to "About This CD-ROM" for more information.

About the Author

Mary Riggs Cohen, Ph.D., is a graduate of Wake Forest University and received her doctoral training at the Catholic University of America. She received postdoctoral family therapy training at the Philadelphia Child Guidance Center and was a clinical supervisor in the psychology training program there through the University of Pennsylvania. Dr. Cohen is a licensed psychologist in New York and Pennsylvania. She has 30 years of experience working with children, adolescents, adults, and families and has specialized in the treatment of Asperger syndrome for 12 years.

While Clinical Director of the Social Learning Disorders Program of the University of Pennsylvania Psychiatry Department, she developed the Social Skills Seminar for young adults with autism spectrum disorders. The program has been taught year round at the University of Pennsylvania and at various locations in the Philadelphia metropolitan area for more than 8 years and most recently in New York City. Her Pennsylvania clinical practice is at the Center for Neuropsychology and Counseling in Warrington. She is an associate of the Asperger Center for Education and Training in New York and has her New York clinical practice at Spectrum Services in Manhattan. Dr. Cohen is a consultant to several schools and autism programs as well as colleges that provide specialized services for students on the spectrum.

Preface

For many individuals with social learning disorders the social world remains a "black box" that is incomprehensible and confusing and a source of frustration in their daily lives. Although some retreat from social gatherings and avoid social contact, there are a great number of individuals who seek to understand social behavior and long for interpersonal connections. Although people with Asperger syndrome and people with social anxiety are often portrayed as aloof and uncaring, those who know them are aware that this is an inaccurate (and unfair) characterization. There are many who desire social contact but do not know how to initiate or maintain relationships. Tired of their solitary existence and isolation, they try to gain insight into the mystifying social behaviors of "neurotypicals."

In 2003, I was asked by colleagues at the University of Pennsylvania to develop a program to teach young adults with Asperger syndrome how to increase their social awareness and gain a better understanding of the social world around them. The result was the Social Skills Seminar, a 12-week course that met weekly for 3 hours. With few models to draw upon, the curriculum was created, to a great extent, through trial and error. Some training methods were research based, whereas others were developed from knowledge of the learning styles of people with Asperger syndrome, high-functioning autism, and nonverbal learning disorders (NLDs). Since then, approximately 240 men and women with Asperger syndrome, high-functioning autism, NLDs, and social anxiety have participated in this program in Philadelphia and New York City. As the course has developed, there have been many opportunities to learn what works and does not work with the participants. The instructors and social coaches who have contributed to the development of the course have helped me to evaluate the successful components of the program over the years.

Social skills training programs have often been found to be ineffective because only basic instrumental skills (e.g., eye contact, greeting) are taught. Individuals must "understand social norms and develop more sophisticated social cognition skills," which are essential to the development of interpersonal relationships and achieving social success (Geller, 2009, p. 32). Adults with Asperger syndrome are often told to smile and make eye contact, but no one has explained to them the rationale for these behaviors. Moreover, the approach to adults has been to modify existing programs used for children and adolescents rather than to address the unique demands of adult social development. As a result, many adults with social learning disorders view social skills training as juvenile, a repeat of what they already know, and inappropriate for their current social needs. There is a critical need for social skills training that is geared to adults who have acquired some basic skills but need to progress to the complexities of dealing with co-workers, establishing romantic relationships, and discovering the social norms of college life and the workplace. It is also essential that social skills be taught in an intellectually stimulating fashion, drawing from current research in the various scientific disciplines that study social behavior.

The Social Skills Seminar program incorporates these critical elements in an interesting and interactive format over 12 weeks of 3-hour sessions. Although the program was initially designed for participants with Asperger syndrome, it has been used successfully with participants with diagnoses of high-functioning autism, NLD, and social phobia. The program focuses on communication skills, recognition of nonverbal communication, job interview skills, and interpersonal skills (friendship, dating, sexuality). An experiential approach is employed in which participants are observed through a one-way mirror while role-playing common social situations they might encounter outside the classroom. There is an emphasis on feedback and support so that each participant is given encouragement to improve his or her social skill repertoire. Most of the classes have had 6–10 participants who were young adult males and females (younger than 30 years); there were also a few older participants. The participants lived in the Philadelphia metropolitan area (including New Jersey and Delaware) and, most recently, in the New York metropolitan area. The education level ranged from college-bound high school graduates to graduate students, and the majority of participants were college graduates (complete demographics information can be found in Chapter 9).

It is acknowledged that the population that participated in this program was high-functioning in general and not representative of all individuals with the diagnoses of Asperger syndrome, high-functioning autism, NLD, or social phobia. Much of the literature regarding adults with more severe impairments, such as Dr. Patricia Howlin's study (Howlin & Yates, 1999), does not reflect the positive outcomes that have been reported for this program's participants. The program is typically conducted in an outpatient setting and, therefore, is not accessible to those with more severe disabilities. Although the target group was college students, the program can be modified to meet the needs of various populations by eliminating more complex aspects of the curriculum (e.g., Internet dating, career selection) or focusing on areas most relevant to a particular group. An additional goal is to expand the program to include more female participants. The ratio of males to females with Asperger syndrome is 8:1; however, research data suggests that social phobia is more prevalent in females (Heimberg & Becker, 2002). Up to this point, only 13% of the program's participants have been female.

Many people with social learning disorders could benefit from this program as past participants have. Our research has indicated that the program reduces social anxiety and increases social motivation for most participants. These two factors are fundamental in breaking the cycle of social isolation and social avoidance that many are experiencing. Since 2003, it has been gratifying to see these individuals achieve a sense of social literacy, thereby improving their self-image and becoming a part of the social world around them.

References

Geller, L. (2009, Summer). Making inclusion work for students with Asperger syndrome. *Autism Spectrum News, 1*, 32–42.

Heimberg, R.G., & Becker, R.E. (2002). *Cognitive behavioral group therapy for social phobia.* New York: Guilford Publishers.

Howlin, P., & Yates, P. (1999). The potential effectiveness of social skills groups for adults with autism. *Autism: International Journal of Research and Practice, 3,* 299–307.

Acknowledgments

Many have contributed to the development of this program. Dr. Anthony Rostain, Dr. Russell Ramsay, Dr. Edward Brodkin, and Dr. Katherine Dahlsgaard—my colleagues at the University of Pennsylvania Department of Psychiatry—provided their expertise in autism spectrum research and clinical interventions. I thank them for their insight and encouragement. I also thank Dr. Lynda Geller, Director of the Asperger Center for Education and Training, for her help in bringing the program to New York City.

Over the last 8 years many individuals have given their time as social coaches, providing support, guidance, and a new social perspective to our participants. I thank Dr. Emily Tinsley, Sarah Lichter, Kait Yulman, Olanrewaju Dokun, Geena Sankoorikal, Kristina Alfaro, Caitlin Howarth, Andrew Chen, Avash Kalra, Ankush Kalra, Isabelle Rostain, Dr. Carolyn Solzhenitzyn, Tyler Dowling, Brandon Kirsch, Steve Yanger, Vikram Prasad, Jodi Yarnell, Dr. Jee Hyun Kim, Dr. John Ceccatti, Robin Chand, David Singer, Paige Weinger, Jeremy Fuhrman, Renee Soufer, David Chang, Rhea Hooper, Caroline Haimm, Debbie Silverman, Carole Kornsweig, Jessica MacDonald, and Megan Daney.

The class has been taught by Dr. Lisa Mimmo, Jodi Yarnell, Dr. Michele Robins, Dr. Carol Moog, Parin Patel, Lisa Ney, Olanrewaju Dokun, Isabelle Rostain, Tyler Dowling, and Geena Sankoorikal. Brandon Kirsch, Tyler Dowling, Jeremy Fuhrman, Renee Soufer, Paige Weinger, and Robin Chand have been invaluable as teaching assistants. Tyler Dowling and Isabelle Rostain have been diligent and innovative co-instructors for three semesters. Finally, this program owes much of its success to the tireless dedication, creativity, and inspiration provided by Geena Sankoorikal and Olanrewaju Dokun.

To my husband, Marvin,
and daughter, Lenore,
for your love and support

Introduction

Foundations of the Social Skills Seminar

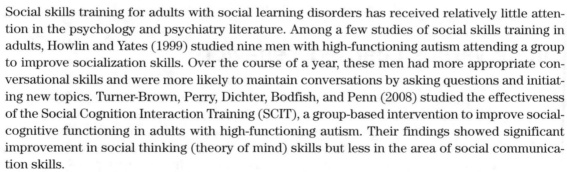Social skills training for adults with social learning disorders has received relatively little attention in the psychology and psychiatry literature. Among a few studies of social skills training in adults, Howlin and Yates (1999) studied nine men with high-functioning autism attending a group to improve socialization skills. Over the course of a year, these men had more appropriate conversational skills and were more likely to maintain conversations by asking questions and initiating new topics. Turner-Brown, Perry, Dichter, Bodfish, and Penn (2008) studied the effectiveness of the Social Cognition Interaction Training (SCIT), a group-based intervention to improve social-cognitive functioning in adults with high-functioning autism. Their findings showed significant improvement in social thinking (theory of mind) skills but less in the area of social communication skills.

Research materials have been developed to train high-functioning adults with autism such as the *Mind Reading* interactive DVD (Golan & Baron-Cohen, 2006), which enhances the ability to "read" faces and emotions, and the Strange Stories Test, which looks at social understanding (Happé, 1994). Although these interventions may be of value, there has been no long-term evaluation of the effectiveness of these methods. Moreover, these interventions are not geared toward day-to-day social interactions, which are particularly problematic for people with social learning disorders.

It is evident that there are a significant number of adults who struggle with the social demands of everyday life. Some of these individuals have been diagnosed with Asperger syndrome, high-functioning autism, social phobia, or nonverbal learning disorder (NLD), but many remain unrecognized. Some may present with only a "shadow syndrome" of autism or anxiety disorder, meaning they do not meet full diagnostic criteria (Ratey & Johnson, 1997). Because they have higher functional abilities than some people with related disorders, they often "fall between the cracks" diagnostically. However, these are the very individuals who struggle with the social demands of life with a hidden disability. Adults who contact the Penn Social Learning Disorders Program at the University of Pennsylvania School of Medicine have often self-diagnosed by reading descriptions of Asperger syndrome online. They are often relieved to receive a diagnosis of Asperger syndrome because it helps explain their lifelong struggle trying to "fit in."

The transition to adulthood often creates a crisis period for these individuals. For those who enter college, there is a sudden loss or absence of structure and nurturance that they may have had at home. In addition, the special education supports that were in place in elementary, middle, and high school are gone and students must reveal their disability and self-advocate. The social demands of college and dormitory life, coupled with an unstructured environment, often lead to negative outcomes for individuals on the autism spectrum. Many of these students drop out or fail their first year. When interviewed, they report the increased social pressure of college as the single issue that created their greatest stress.

Another common scenario is the high-achieving graduate who cannot find employment due to poor social skills that severely hinder performance in the job interview process. Such individuals are often underemployed and unsatisfied with the low-skilled positions they are forced to take (Fast, 2004). Many are lonely and would like to develop interpersonal or romantic relationships but have never had close friendships and have never dated.

Experience in the Penn Social Learning Disorders Program has indicated that the early twenties often form a critical period of adjustment for individuals with social learning disorders. A 2005 study of adults on the autism spectrum found that they identified maintaining personal relationships, relationships at work, and dealing with the opposite sex as major social challenges (Sperry & Mesibov, 2005). The program developed a seminar that aims to address the life transition issues that young adults are encountering: college life, employment, and developing interpersonal relationships. This book and its accompanying CD-ROM outline the Social Skills Seminar, which can be used to help young adults in these areas.

Innate versus Learned Behavior

Many people assume that social behavior is not learned and develops naturally. Darwin (1871) thought that nonverbal signals were innate. Conversely, cultural anthropologists (La Barre, 1947) view nonverbal behavior as learned through social participation. The Social Skills Seminar recognizes the role of both genetic and environmental learning factors in shaping social behaviors. There is clearly a strong genetic component to predisposition to autism spectrum disorders (ASDs) as well as other social learning disorders (Cederlund & Gillberg, 2004; Piven, Palmer, Jacobi, Childress, & Arndt, 1997). Gene variants that affect brain development and functioning are likely to affect many aspects of an individual's social behavior. However, social behaviors are not determined by genetics alone, as many crucial aspects of social behavior are learned through years of interaction with family members, neighbors, or peers.

The neurobiological differences seen in an individual with social learning disorder contribute to his or her difficulties learning social cues. Although some aspects of social behavior, such as the facial expression of emotion, appear to be more genetically determined or "hardwired" (Ekman, 2003), the interpretation of facial expressions seems to be a more learned response. Understanding the complexities of social behavior requires many years of observation and experience, both of which are difficult for those with social learning disorders because they are not oriented to observing people and have little social experience to draw upon. Many have led a very solitary existence, which only contributes to their lack of understanding. They avoid social settings such as parties, concerts, or other outings that would provide them the experience that they lack. Consequently, as their avoidance continues, their social isolation is perpetuated.

The treatment philosophy presented here is that social behavior such as understanding nonverbal cues or conversation skills can be learned, to a great extent, even in adulthood. This is why the term *social learning disorders* was chosen to describe the individuals who can benefit from the Social Skills Seminar. The purpose of this program is to provide a detailed approach to social skills acquisition that is designed for individuals with specific social learning disorders and addresses their unique learning styles. In essence, this program strives to teach "social literacy" to enable individuals with social learning disorders to read and comprehend social behavior.

Those with social learning disorders have difficulty understanding nonverbal social cues, such as body language and "reading" facial expressions. These impairments cause them to be uncertain of how to respond to others and lead them to make social blunders, such as not knowing when to enter a conversation or not knowing when to stop talking. Adults with social learning disorders often do not pick up important social cues and therefore do not know how to respond to others. Also, they may fail to recognize the other person's expression of discomfort with a particular topic and continue to talk about it. Many adults with social learning disorders have literal interpretations of conversations, which cause them great misunderstanding. They do not understand idioms (e.g., "think outside the box") or metaphors (e.g., "rolling in dough") or imprecise language. As a consequence, they must be taught not to have expectations when people make broad statements such as "I'll call you the middle of next week." Otherwise, an individual with social learning disorder may be very upset if he or she is not contacted on Wednesday. This person must learn that most people speak nonspecifically or in generalities and sometimes make promises, out of politeness, that they do not intend to keep.

Generalization of Skills

One criticism of traditional social skills programs is that although the specific skills of eye contact, body language, and conversation are acquired by repeated practice, these often do not transfer to the everyday situations encountered (Howlin, 2004). Indeed, many of the participants understood these basic skills. However, they continued to have difficulty establishing and maintaining social relationships. The primary difficulty they reported was the inability to understand other people's intentions, motivations, or point of view.

The Social Skills Seminar has sought to bridge the gap between the classroom and real-life experience through the use of social coaches, who were trained to give concise feedback regarding particular social behaviors. Social coaches provided an experiential component to what was learned in the class and accompanied participants to certain social activities each week (e.g., going to a bookstore, coffee bar, or restaurant). The coaches supported the participants in carrying out particular social "exercises," such as observing other people's interactions and making inferences about relationship and interactions based on nonverbal cues. As such, coaches served as facilitators and provided feedback and support. Some also helped participants reduce their anxiety by utilizing relaxation exercises and gradual exposure to social settings.

All the social coaches in the Social Skills Seminar have been postbaccalaureate or graduate students in social work, psychology, or psychiatry residents. Some had prior training in working with individuals on the autism spectrum, and all received training prior to working in the program. They were relatively close in age to the class participants, which also provided an experience of peer acceptance. The social coaches served as role models of appropriate behavior. It is essential that anyone providing social coaching exhibit maturity, social awareness, and personal integrity.

Understanding the Social Brain

Human behavior, thoughts, and emotions, like those of other primates, are generally highly oriented towards social interactions. Studies of primates (Dunbar, 1992) have suggested that human societal advances are mostly a result of improved social communication. Dunbar (1992) hypothesized a relationship between primate group size and degree of brain development. As a social group increases in size, its increased complexity creates a demand for more developed social cognitive skills. Over time, humans have developed the ability to perceive and communicate mental states such as beliefs and desires. This ability to "mentalize" is virtually absent in other primates and is underdeveloped in individuals on the autism spectrum (Frith, 2003; Premack & Woodruff, 1978).

Most children are able to mentalize by 4–6 years of age, as evidenced by their ability to understand the hidden puppet task (a theory of mind task). A puppet is placed in a blue cabinet and then changed to a red cabinet after one person leaves the room. The children are aware that the person absent from the room has a false belief about the location of the puppet and can predict that the person will look in the blue cabinet for the puppet (Avis & Harris, 1991). In contrast, children with autism spectrum disorders do not understand this distinction and perceive everyone to be operating with the same information. They are not aware that different people have different thoughts, which translates into problems with joint attention, pretend play, and the ability to understand any kind of deception (Happé, 1994). Although children with ASDs improve their mentalizing ability over time, it continues to be a problem area that impedes social understanding. In adults, the lack of mentalizing causes misperceptions of others' behavior and the consequent inappropriate responses. An illustration of this is a young man who could not understand why people in his class would not reveal who wrote inappropriate comments on the board while the instructor was out. After blurting out the name of the student who played the prank, he could not understand why the other members of the class were very annoyed with him.

Neural Pathways

Advances in neuroscience have begun to elucidate the brain pathways that mediate social behaviors and that are disrupted in ASDs (Courchesne & Pierce, 2005). Humans' social skills have evolved to help them adapt to the environment and improve their lot in life. Success depends on the ability to influence, cooperate with, and understand other people. Much of this is learned over time, but some social behaviors—such as the fundamental interest in interacting with others, the development of the social smile, and so on—seem to be innate and clearly rooted in the biology of the brain (Ratey, 2001). Repeated practice can strengthen social skills, presumably by modifying neural pathways that mediate social perception and social behaviors. A person who has social difficulties due to a neurobiological condition, such as Asperger syndrome or NLD, can learn new ways of being socially appropriate. Eye contact, body proximity, and facial recognition are examples of behaviors that are either innate or acquired naturally and that are often impaired in people with social learning disorders. These individuals can learn through repetition to compensate for these impairments. The strengthening of the neural connections continues with practice until the behavior becomes a part of their repertoire.

Structural Differences

Figure 1 illustrates the structure of the brain. This material is referenced throughout the following section.

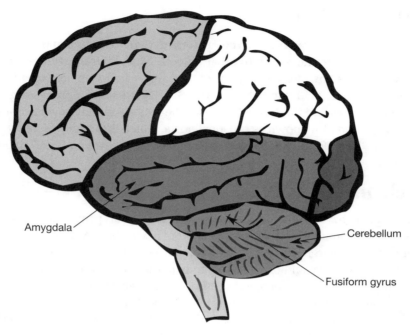

Figure 1. Structure of the human brain.

Cerebellum

The cerebellum appears to play a vital role in social interaction. It coordinates input from the senses and sustains attention. These abilities are critical to meaningful "coherent" social encounters. One must pay attention and have the ability to shift attention between others' behaviors, verbalizations, or facial expressions for meaningful interaction to occur (Ratey, 2001). These abilities are often compromised for those with social learning disorders. These individuals must develop focused attention on people rather than things. As Baron-Cohen suggested, they are more interested in how things work (systematizing) than how people feel and behave (empathizing). In addition, individuals with social learning disorders must learn to coordinate the incoming social information and develop an appropriate response. This requires much practice and concentration. Social scripts often help initially in socially difficult situations such as meeting new people or going to a party.

Amygdala

The amygdala plays a central role in mediating social anxiety. When an individual is anxious in a social situation, the amygdala is activated and arousal is heightened, sometimes leading to a cycle of increasing and overwhelming fear. These types of experiences only reinforce and strengthen the phobia (Goleman, 1995). Neuroimaging studies of people with social phobia have shown a marked reactivity to social cues occurring in the amygdala (Stein, Goldin, Sareen, Zorilla, & Brown, 2002). Conversely, when an individual has a calming experience, such as someone speaking in a soothing voice or reassuring with a gentle touch on the arm, the panic reaction can sometimes be prevented or stopped (Ratey, 2001).

Fusiform Face Area

The fusiform face area (part of the fusiform gyrus) is the area of the brain that processes faces. It responds more to faces than to other objects. Nine different studies have reported that individuals with ASDs have less activation of this area when viewing faces (Schultz, 2005). Dr Robert Schultz has indicated that people with ASDs use the object processing region of the brain when looking at faces and therefore do not see them as something special. Some individuals with ASDs display a condition known as prosopagnosia, which is the total inability to recognize faces. Many people with NLDs and ASDs cannot remember faces (Attwood, 2007; Liddell & Rasmussen, 2005).

Whole Brain Theory

Researchers have posited that those with ASDs do not "prune" unnecessary neurons in their early years of development, which results in them having larger brains. Dr. Nancy Minshew of the University of Pittsburgh has investigated size variations in white matter, limbic structures, corpus callosum, cerebellum, and brain stem and hypothesizes that individuals with ASDs have a disorder of complex information processing. Many social behaviors, such as conversation, require this type of complex processing that involves interconnections throughout the brain (Minshew & Williams, 2007). This can explain why individuals with ASDs often seem rigid in their social behavior and slow to adapt to different situations.

Cognitive Style

It appears that there is a particular cognitive style present in most people with social learning disorders. This includes weak central coherence (Happé, 2006), or the ability to attend to detail but miss "the big picture" or overall context. An individual with a social learning disorder may notice a particular item of clothing (e.g., a T-shirt logo) worn by a person but entirely miss the social interaction (an argument) going on between that person and the others present. Executive functioning (problem solving, planning, initiation) impairments are also common. As a result, these individuals struggle with complex social situations that require them to think of and execute an appropriate response. The combination of these cognitive elements requires that social information be explained in a concise manner with specific courses of action recommended for specific situations. Otherwise, these individuals will not be able to integrate the details into the larger context and initiate an appropriate course of action.

Researchers have discovered that individuals with ASDs detect fewer social cues when using procedures such as the Social Attribution Task (SAT). The SAT employs silent cartoon animation in which geometric shapes act out a social plot (the shapes chase, fight, entrap, play, and get frightened). The neurotypical subjects created narratives that attributed social meaning to the cartoon, whereas the people with ASDs identified only 25% of the social elements in the story. Neurotypical individuals will use their knowledge of social relationships to attribute meaning to an "ambiguous visual display," but individuals with ASDs do not personify the shapes in the film, instead relying on physical relationships in their descriptions (Klin, 2000). This illustrates why a person with an ASD misses important social information and then cannot respond appropriately to the situation. This supports the emphasis placed on teaching increased awareness of social cues by stressing the importance of observation exercises such as those that have been incorporated into the Social Skills Seminar.

Mirror Neurons

The discovery of mirror neurons in monkeys (Rizzolatti, Fadiga, Gallese, & Fogassi, 1996) has led to the revelation that a large portion of the human motor system is activated when observing actions in others (Blakemore, Winston, & Frith, 2004). Giacomo Rizzolati and his associates discovered certain neurons that respond when monkeys see someone else performing an action as well as when they perform the action themselves. The study of mirror neurons attempts to identify the brain mechanisms involved in the ability to understand one's own and another person's actions. It appears that this ability is crucial to understanding others' intentions and to imitation of behavior. These mechanisms, in turn, are fundamental to higher level social processes such as empathy.

The direct form of understanding others that is called intentional attunement (Gallese, 2006) occurs when social stimuli are observed and internal representations of the body states associated with actions emotions and sensations are evoked in the observer. It is as if the observer were doing a similar action or experiencing a similar emotion or sensation. A study by Tager-Flusberg (2005) showed that the mirror neurons of individuals with ASDs were less activated when watching human movement than those of neurotypical adults (Dingfelder, 2005). Theories regarding the brain's mirroring system suggests that faulty mirror neurons may be involved in social dysfunction and even repetitive behaviors such as hand flapping (Oberman & Ramachandran, 2007).

Despite these neurophysiologic differences, people with social disorders can overcome their impairments with compensatory learning. The teaching of social rules must be explicit (Frith, 2004) for individuals to make the necessary adaptations in their behavior. Dr. Tager-Flusberg (2005), who has researched mirror neurons, suggests that behavioral treatments could be developed to retrain neurons or help individuals with autism spectrum disorders develop compensatory systems (Dingfelder, 2005). In response to current views of social cognition and the importance of imitation in the development of empathy, the Social Skills Seminar emphasizes observation of social behavior, rehearsal (imitation) of those behaviors, and experience using the behaviors in a variety of settings. The social coaches are instrumental in creating these experiences and therefore in the participants' developing new compensatory social behaviors.

Gender Differences

Although all adults with social learning disorders have certain commonalities in their inability to effectively read social cues, gender differences do exist. In general, women are seen as being more socially "attuned," and this is true of females with social learning disorders as well. For example, Dr. Tony Attwood has observed that women with Asperger syndrome imitate their peers more than males, which gives them the appearance of being socially competent (Attwood, 2007). Liane Willey, a woman with Asperger syndrome, writes that she had an uncanny ability to imitate others' expressions, gestures, and accents. She used her gift for imitation to camouflage her social difficulties (Willey, 1999).

Many of the women with Asperger syndrome who participated in the Penn Social Skills Program said that they are generally more comfortable with men than with other women. This is possibly because they are not as adept at emotional expression, which is the glue of most female friendships. Another factor is the complexity of female social behavior and its subtleties. Anyone who remembers the female cliques of middle school and high school will acknowledge how female aggression is subtle but cruel at times. Women with Asperger syndrome are often bewildered by the subtle deceptiveness of female social behavior (e.g., pretending to be someone's friend while spreading rumors about her) and find it difficult to play the game (Attwood, 2007). One young woman in the program described how she never understood why girls in her college dorm were making "catty remarks" about each other and then hanging out together later. Dr. Attwood has found that girls and women with Asperger syndrome suffer more socially than boys and men who have the syndrome (Attwood, 2007).

Recognizing and Emphasizing Strengths

Over the years, the instructors and social coaches have often been struck by the exceptionality and immense potential of many of the program participants. There are a significant number who have artistic talent, are musically gifted, or have a facility with languages. One young woman with Asperger syndrome had taught herself four Middle Eastern languages and regional Indian dialects. A young man was a gifted sculptor who later received a prestigious scholarship to an arts college. Another, who was a graphic artist, was later hired by a major magazine. There have been many participants who were animators, video game designers, science fiction writers, or cartoonists. The examples are numerous and are supported by the view that artistic skills are relatively more common in those with ASDs (Gillberg, 2006). In his book *The Genesis of Artistic Creativity: Asperger Syndrome and the Arts*, Michael Fitzgerald (2005) notes that many with ASDs have a special ability that allows them to separate an object into its component parts, which is especially significant in painting and drawing. He postulates that many well-known writers, artists, and philosophers were individuals on the spectrum who had the ability to view the world from a unique perspective. Others such as Donna Williams (1998) have suggested that those on the autism spectrum have a special type of heightened sensing that neurotypical individuals lack, which contributes to their creativity. They also have an ability to hyperfocus on their area of interest and form unusual associations. There are a number of creative individuals with this unique perspective who struggle to fit into the conventional world and are particularly confused by their social surroundings. It is important to recognize the talents that can accompany social learning disorders and incorporate these abilities in the Social Skills Seminar environment. Artists are always encouraged to bring in their artwork. One class had a number of musicians who all brought their instruments and played together for the other participants. In this way, their skills were employed in a social activity that could be shared by all.

A Work in Progress

Since its inception in 2003, the Social Skills Seminar has approached the social skills training of adults as continually evolving. With few models to draw upon, the curriculum was created, to a great extent, through trial and error. Some training methods were research based, such as viewing silent movies to learn nonverbal communication (Gray, 2004) or using the Micro Expression Training Tool (Ekman, 2003). Others were developed from the knowledge that those working in the Penn Social Learning Disorders Program had of the visual learning styles of individuals with social learning disorders. In working with these individuals, it was realized that visual feedback images are often essential for their learning of social behaviors, which led to initiating the use of a one-way mirror and videotaping as teaching tools. For these adults, social behaviors must be viewed repeatedly and then analyzed. The exercises in this program attempt to retrain their eyes to become more aware of nonverbal cues and to retrain their ears to listen carefully to what is being verbalized.

In 2005, the addition of social coaches expanded the experiential component of the program by providing opportunities for individualized skills practice in a variety of settings. The participants practiced conversations, interviews, and nonverbal communication exercises with their coaches on a weekly basis. This reinforced the skills taught in class and provided a more individualized approach to each participant's specific social impairments.

Individuals with social learning disorders are typically seeking concrete guidelines for complex social behaviors such as dating and job interviewing. Although it is often difficult to provide hard-and-fast rules for these kinds of situations, this program has attempted to provide general guidelines for behavior based on current sources (Internet resources, articles, books, and descriptions of current dating mores by social coaches, who are in the same age range as participants). The complexity of the social world creates such anxiety for adults with social learning disorders that it seems appropriate to provide these supports.

The caveat to these social guidelines is that there are always exceptions to the typical social mores. How a person behaves in a dating situation is not predictable. Employers tend to ask certain questions in a job interview, but there is no way to predict exactly what will occur with a particular interviewer. There are specific topics (e.g., religion, politics) that it is generally wise to avoid in conversations with strangers, but there may be other topics that would be offensive to certain individuals. These discrepancies will always exist in the complex world of social interaction. The approach of this program has been to provide the most generally accepted behavioral strategies. The handouts containing these suggestions and strategies may be found in the class outlines at the ends of Chapters 4–7.

Feedback

Feedback from participants was a key element in determining what aspects of the training were effective in addressing their needs. One example was the participants' request for a simulated party to practice their conversation skills. They wanted to experience being in a party atmosphere and learn how to initiate or join ongoing conversations. This type of experiential exercise was also helpful in reducing anxiety because support was readily available if somebody felt uncomfortable.

Participants were asked to evaluate the training at the end of each session and indicate what aspects of the training worked for them and what should be revised or eliminated. They were also asked to evaluate themselves on two social responsiveness measures—the Friendship Questionnaire (Baron-Cohen & Wheelwright, 2003) and the Empathy Quotient (Baron-Cohen & Wheelwright, 2004)—prior to the training and after. Parents were asked to fill out the Social Responsiveness Scale–Adult Version (Costantino et al., 2003) prior to the course and at a 3-month interval after the course was completed. In addition, participants evaluated their social coaches using a Coaches Evaluation (see the end of Chapter 3). Utilizing these methods, the program has been continually reformulated and refined. Experience indicates that it will continue to develop as the population served grows and diversifies.

1

Understanding Social Learning Disorders

> The sophistication of our mind-reading skills is part of our heritage as social primates; our biology contains cheat sheets for building theories about other minds because our brains evolved—and continue to evolve—in complex social environments where being able to outfox or cooperate with your fellow humans was essential.
>
> Steven Johnson (2004)

An individual with a social learning disorder is anyone who meets the diagnostic criteria for Asperger syndrome, an ASD, nonverbal learning disorder, or social anxiety. Each of these diagnoses indicates a core impairment in social functioning. People who exhibit social learning disorders often display a wide range of functioning, which can make the diagnosis difficult. Many are employed; some are married and have families. Some higher functioning individuals have mastered basic social skills, such as eye contact, voice inflection, and attention to nonverbal cues (social perception). However, they may have a minor form of "mindblindness," in that they cannot understand the feelings, beliefs, and motivations for other people's behavior. Their abilities to intuit emotional states are limited. Therefore, they cannot anticipate other people's behavior, and they have difficulty "mentalizing." Although certain aspects of mentalizing can be learned, taking another person's perspective remains effortful (Frith, 2005).

The distinction between *social perception* and *social cognition* was made by Tager-Flusberg (2001), who argued that social perception is the main impairment seen in Asperger syndrome. *Social perception* can be defined as the process by which an individual infers other people's motives and intentions from observing their behavior. People with social phobia also exhibit perceptual differences by their negative bias to social situations (e.g., only noticing faces with unfriendly rather than friendly expressions). Although adults with social learning disorders can often make

11

appropriate responses in a laboratory setting, they have difficulty in real-life situations, which are more complex and require quick responses to often ambiguous situations (Frith, 2004). Participants in social skills seminars can often arrive at a correct response, given enough time, by using logic. However, this ability does not translate well to the social world, where cues must be processed quickly.

The *Diagnostic and Statistical Manual of Mental Disorders, Fourth Edition, Text Revision* (*DSM-IV-TR*; American Psychiatric Association [APA], 2000) criteria for a diagnosis of Asperger's Disorder includes impairment in social interaction and social communication. Similarly, a diagnosis of Social Phobia includes a marked fear of social interaction that causes an anxiety response (APA, 2000). Nonverbal learning disorder, although not classified as a distinct diagnosis in the *DSM-IV-TR*, is a neurological condition that is typified by poor social interaction, poor social judgment, and difficulty with social communication (Rourke, 1995). Each of these diagnoses comprise the group referred to as having a social learning disorder.

Employment Issues

Individuals with social learning disorders typically have patterns of repeated termination from employment and difficulty with co-workers. They do not understand office politics and make continual mistakes in their dealings with employers and co-workers. Moreover, they are frequently unaware of their blunders and bewildered when they are reprimanded by a supervisor. When terminated, they often do not receive feedback from their employers and continue their inappropriate behaviors in other employment settings. A common complaint of individuals with social learning disorders is that no one tells them what they are doing wrong. As with other assumptions about social behavior, the employers often do not feel this degree of explanation is needed.

Marital Discord/Family Disconnect

An adult may seek social skills training because his or her spouse is complaining about withdrawal or disconnection from the family. These adults may spend long periods of time engaged in solitary activities, not participating in family life (e.g., playing computer games solo while the rest of the family enjoys a game night together). They may not be comfortable with family vacations or socializing with extended family during holidays. They may feel that they are as involved as necessary from their perspective.

A person with a social learning disorder may not actively seek out social opportunities because of feelings of social inadequacy. Family members may misinterpret their behavior as rejection or simply not caring. Adults with social learning disorders may be perceived as self-absorbed and egocentric because of their tendency to prefer solitary pursuits. In reality, they are often just overwhelmed by the demands of social situations and have little confidence in their abilities to be successful in social settings.

Communication Difficulties

Adults with social learning disorders often develop negative self-images in relation to socializing. They may perceive themselves as boring because they have difficulty maintaining conversations. In reality, they may have a wealth of interesting information to share but lack knowledge of the mechanics of conversation. They may interrupt or monopolize conversations because they do not understand the natural, reciprocal back-and-forth rhythm of conversing. Their discomfort may cause them to talk too rapidly or not pause for the other person's response. As a result, the dialogue may quickly evolve into a monologue, causing the other party to feel ignored, cut off the conversation, or simply walk away.

Conversational mechanics do not come easily to individuals with social learning disorders. They may require repeated practice to develop a sense of rhythm and an understanding of issues such as topic transition and balance between speakers. Furthermore, impairments in theory of mind (the ability to think about another's thoughts) may cause individuals with social learning disorders to start conversations in midstream because their assumption is that the other person knows what they are talking about. It may be difficult for individuals with social learning disorders to understand that people do not automatically follow their thought patterns. Their limited ability to see other people's perspectives may cause them to appear self-centered and self-serving. However, they need these different perspectives to act in a more empathic manner. Although adults with social learning disorders are often described as uncaring by co-workers, peers, or family members, it is their lack of awareness and understanding of other people's feelings that causes them to appear this way.

Sensory Issues

Adults with social learning disorders may appear awkward or ill at ease with their bodies. Sensory issues can interfere with their perceptions of their bodies and their relationships to others. For example, individuals with social learning disorders may not realize that they are standing too close to another person who, as a result, is feeling uncomfortable. Conversely, they may position themselves too far from a group to be perceived as being part of it. Individuals with social learning disorders thus may be seen as outsiders before they even attempt to interact.

Individuals with social learning disorders may not orient their bodies toward their conversational partners, which can cause confusion about to whom they are speaking. During observations of classroom participants, individuals with social learning disorders were either "in the face" of the other students or not aligned toward people with whom they were trying to initiate a conversation. A common response from other students was, "Are you talking to me?"

Another perceptual impairment found in some individuals with social learning disorders is the phenomena of prosopagnosia, or "face-blindness." Individuals with prosopagnosia have difficulty recognizing people's faces unless they have seen them many times before, which inevitably causes social awkwardness and interferes with the ability to maintain relationships. Some people rely on other methods for recognition, such as looking at a person's clothing, gait, or movements. It appears that prosopagnosia is related to abnormal perceptual processing of the face (Bogdashina, 2003). That is, individuals with prosopagnosia do not process the face as a whole but tend to focus on specific features (e.g., the hairline, chin). This impairment also affects their abilities to recognize facial expression of emotions.

In addition to their hyposensitivity or lack of response to certain types of environmental stimuli, individuals with social learning disorders often experience hypersensitivity to sound, touch, texture, and light. They are often distracted by some kinds of environmental stimuli, which they find difficult to ignore. These issues may have implications for their social behaviors, such as avoiding crowded or noisy activities. Many individuals with social learning disorders do not enjoy parties because they find the environment to be overstimulating. These individuals may not respond well to large groups because of the degree of sensory distraction that they cannot suppress.

Language Processing Impairments

Another characteristic of individuals with social learning disorders is their literal interpretation of language, which contributes to perpetual misunderstandings in social situations. For example, if a woman gives an excuse for not accepting a date and is not direct about not being interested, a man with a social learning disorder will typically continue to ask her out multiple times. Adults with social learning disorders do not understand the typical dating games or mating rituals of our society. The nonverbal nature of flirtation is often overlooked or misinterpreted. Individuals with social learning disorders expect direct answers instead of coyness or manipulation; therefore, they may be bewildered by dating and relationships in general. Some of their attempts at establishing romantic relationships are inappropriate and may even be perceived as stalking.

Individuals with social learning disorders may request social guidelines for their behavior to minimize the complexities of social interaction and provide a template for their actions (Ramsay et al., 2005). Although it may be difficult to simplify these interactions, it has been useful in teaching the social skills seminars to provide conversation guidelines, dating guidelines, and job interview guidelines to reduce anxiety and provide structure to an ambiguous situation. The guidelines should have a brief, direct format that fits the cognitive style of adults with social learning disorders, who often need concise suggestions that do not require in-depth analysis. They often prefer a logical rationale for behavior; for example, "Making eye contact is positive because most people like for you to look at them, and it makes them feel acknowledged." Another way to explain social norms is to take an anthropological viewpoint: "Humans and primates view standing in close proximity as a threatening behavior." Adults with social learning disorders are frequently well educated and appreciate a more scientific approach to understanding the social world.

Attention-Deficit/Hyperactivity Disorder or Attention-Deficit Disorder

A significant number of individuals with social learning disorders are also diagnosed with attention-deficit/hyperactivity disorder (ADHD) or attention-deficit disorder (ADD). A study by Anckarsäter et al. (2006) found that of 113 adults diagnosed with an ASD, 49 were also diagnosed with ADHD. Attention problems may lead to fragmented perceptions of the environment and, consequently, inaccurate social perceptions. The ability to attend to social stimuli is critical in learning social behaviors and adapting to one's environment. Impairments in attention may also lead to the poor central coherence that is often observed in adults with social learning disorders, as well as poor self-monitoring. Central coherence involves the ability to see "the big picture" and not be lost in the details (Anckarsäter et al., 2006).

Achievement/Ability Discrepancy

Adults with social learning disorders may be underemployed with respect to their educational level and intellect, working in low-level jobs that do not meet their potential (Gerhardt, 2008). They may be frustrated by the interviewing process and may not understand how to communicate their skills effectively. Individuals with social learning disorders may be highly qualified but not able to project this in the interview because of their social anxiety and communication impairments. Answering questions such as "What are your weaknesses?" is difficult because they are prone to being overly critical of themselves. Individuals with social learning disorders may not understand how to shape their answers in a positive way or highlight their abilities. Also, their propensity for honesty can send up red flags to a potential employer. For example, when one young man with a social learning disorder was asked to cite a weakness, he said, "I'm not very punctual." Although he was referring to his behaviors outside of work settings, he did not make this clear to the interviewer. This response, which would disqualify the applicant immediately from the perspective of most employers, is an indication that the individual with a social learning disorder does not understand the perspectives of others. It did not occur to this man that an employer would not want to hire a chronically late employee.

Defense Mechanisms

The continual rejection experienced by individuals with social learning disorders may transform their sense of self. They may develop negative images and perceive themselves as failures both in their personal and professional lives. This often leads to self-defeating behaviors. For example, individuals with social learning disorders may sabotage social situations before they have a chance to be rejected (Attwood, 2009). Often their defense mechanism is to assume an uncaring attitude to avoid social rejection. They shield their vulnerability by adopting a negative mind-set to any social activity. Because they often feel like outcasts, they may relate to fringe societal groups. Adolescents might associate with nonconformist groups such as "goths" or even join extreme religious groups to find acceptance. One woman who participated in the program recalled joining the "metalheads" group in high school because they provided a feeling of belonging. In her book *Aquamarine Blue 5*, which chronicles the experiences of college students with Asperger syndrome, Dawn Prince-Hughes (2002) described her struggle to find acceptance in a group. She felt most comfortable with those in the dramatic arts because their behavior was more eccentric than her own.

Many adults with social learning disorders carry the emotional baggage of their adolescence and childhood into their interpersonal relationships. As a result, they may be highly sensitive to criticism from a spouse, co-worker, or friend. The perception of criticism is often present even when a comment is neutral. In turn, individuals with social learning disorders may develop a somewhat paranoid view of the world and anticipate negative social outcomes for themselves. Because of their social naiveté, they may have been duped or set up in their past; now, as a consequence, they may view all potential relationships with suspicion. Not surprisingly, this mind-set often prevents them from establishing positive and satisfying relationships.

Cognitive Rigidity

Social behavior is complex and involves having a repertoire of possible responses to situations. The problem for most adults with social learning disorders is that they have limited responses and often engage in rigid, repetitive behaviors (Attwood, 2007). The cognitive profile of individuals with social learning disorders indicates that adapting to new circumstances may be very difficult because of the rigidity of their thoughts. They may have only one response and cannot easily generate new ones without help. As a result of this cognitive rigidity, individuals with social learning disorders tend to keep employing the same flawed strategies in their social decision making. For example, one student would offend people with his political and ethnic jokes. Although he realized that people were not responding favorably to this behavior, he said he could not think of another way to get attention.

Some individuals with social learning disorders present with an all-knowing, condescending attitude. Because of their cognitive rigidity, these individuals tend to think that their opinion is always right and argue their point of view incessantly. They are unaware that this is irritating and off-putting to others. Because adults with social learning disorders have low self-esteem, they are particularly invested in winning arguments and can come across as defensive, angry, and close-minded. In reality, their bravado masks a poor self-image that comes from years of social rejection.

Difficulty with Deception

Socially appropriate behavior does not mean telling the truth in every situation. Individuals with ASDs tend to view social white lies, which are told to spare another person's feelings, as just being dishonest (Attwood, 2007). It can be difficult to explain to adults with social learning disorders that much of what people say and do in a social context is deceptive: complimenting someone's appearance when it is not really meant or suppressing true opinions about the dinner someone just prepared.

For many adults with social learning disorders, the world is either black or white, with no shades of gray. The tendency to be brutally honest may cause a myriad of social difficulties, which leads to further isolation and social rejection. Comments such as "What's with your hair?" or "You've sure put on a few pounds" do not enhance individuals with social learning disorders in their social spheres.

Poor Self-Image

Adults with social learning disorders may have internalized a very negative image of themselves (Attwood, 2007). They may see themselves as social losers who are boring to others. They may feel awkward and out of place in social situations. In addition, they often have the social anxiety characteristic known as negative bias. They only pick up on negative events and fail to notice positive events such as social overtures from others. For example, a young man with Asperger syndrome talked about his obsession with Godzilla movies and why he related to them:

> I have always seen Godzilla as a sympathetic character. He doesn't belong in this world and as a result everything he does causes problems. He can't even move without crushing something and he is continually filled with frustration and rage. That is how I feel because I don't belong. He and I are very similar except he is powerful and I'm not.

After years of feeling inadequate socially, adults with social learning disorders often have little expectation that their lives will improve. Some have experienced so much rejection that they avoid any social interaction at all. Their loneliness and isolation may contribute to their negative self-image of being unattractive or undesirable and, therefore, incapable of establishing relationships. This mind-set often creates a self-perpetuating cycle of rejection. Individuals with social learning disorders may not anticipate positive outcomes and often sabotage their social encounters by their negative behaviors. For example, they may look aloof by standing at a distance or look depressed by their slumping posture and downcast expression. As previously noted, the signals that they unknowingly send cause others to avoid them. Many times they expect rejection and are surprised when it does not happen. One participant in a social skills program said that he expected women to be afraid of him because he "looks creepy." He was surprised when a woman was receptive to talking with him because he had anticipated the rejection before he initiated the conversation.

Social Anxiety and Substance Abuse

Social anxiety may also result in desperate behaviors such as alcohol and substance abuse. The faulty thinking of some individuals with social learning disorders that drugs and alcohol will help them to fit in better socially usually backfires. Many individuals with social learning disorders report using alcohol to relax but find that their social awareness is even more impaired when under the influence. Students are particularly vulnerable to this behavior during college when the social pressures are great. Individuals with Asperger syndrome have compulsive tendencies, which can lead to overuse of alcohol and other tranquilizing substances (Berney, 2004). These forms of substance abuse may provide a false sense of security to those for whom socializing is awkward and uncomfortable. In reality, their social judgment may be even more impaired while using these substances, and they often find their behavior to be perceived as highly inappropriate.

For this reason, participants in social skills programs should be encouraged to avoid bars as outlets for socializing. Other settings such as coffee shops, bookstores, or music stores offer a more neutral atmosphere for social encounters. Individuals can talk casually with people there and not have the distraction of loud music or large groups. Also, there are fewer assumptions made about a woman talking casually with a man in these settings. There is a variety of subjects available when perusing books, magazines, or movies. Bookstores and coffee shops also provide a more relaxed atmosphere with less sensory stimulation.

Socially Anxious Thoughts

A number of participants in social skills seminars have diagnoses of social anxiety. Fear of socializing is also characteristic of most individuals with ASDs. Cath, Ran, Smit, van Balkdom, and Comijs (2008) used measures specific to social anxiety and found that individuals with ASDs scored similarly to individuals with diagnoses of "pure" social anxiety. Participants in our social skills program typically score high on the Social Interaction Anxiety Scale (Mattick & Clarke, 1998), which is administered during the first class. They may report socially anxious thoughts, such as worrying about being ignored, being perceived as odd, or saying something embarrassing. Cognitive-behavioral therapy (CBT) has been found to be effective in reducing the socially anxious thoughts and avoidance behaviors in individuals with social learning disorders (Chalfant, Rapee, & Carroll, 2007). For this reason, the basic tenets of CBT are incorporated in the social skills seminar.

2

Program Design

The social instinct,
together with sympathy,
is like any other instinct,
greatly strengthened by habit.
Charles Darwin (1871)

Theoretical Foundations of Program Design

Research suggests that social behavior is learned best using modeling, role playing, repetition, and real-life experiences (Ratey, 2001). Therefore, this program was designed to provide practical skills that are consolidated into learned behavior through repeated exercises. The use of social coaches adds a new dimension by providing individualized practice sessions that are tailored to the student's needs. The practice sessions should immediately follow the classroom instruction to reinforce the skills taught while providing support and feedback.

CBT principles are helpful in targeting the negative belief systems that participants have about social experiences. As mentioned, these beliefs become generalized and create self-defeating behaviors such as avoidance. Individuals diagnosed with social anxiety tend to interpret neutral faces as having a negative expression. They tend to remember negative or critical facial expressions better than positive ones and have a tendency to rate themselves critically (Antony & Swinson, 2000b). Many people with social learning disorders anticipate negative actions by other people and therefore make these assumptions about any reaction from others. Cognitive modification methods can be used to revise negative thoughts and adapt them to the social context (Ramsay et al., 2005). This course uses aspects of CBT for individuals with social learning disorders to understand and reshape their thoughts and feelings about social experiences. Many individuals with social anxiety run through a repertoire of negative thoughts automatically in social settings without really paying attention to what is happening in the situation (Stopa & Clark, 2000). Cognitive therapy attempts to break the cycle of negativity and social avoidance by providing strategies for coping with anxiety and learning to control negative thoughts. For example, people with social anxiety tend to engage in all-or-nothing thinking, in which they view a situation as either good or bad, even though most situations have both positive and negative elements. Another common thinking style is known as the mental filter, in which the individual focuses on one negative detail instead of seeing the whole picture (Beck, 1995). By individuals learning to be aware of their maladaptive thinking patterns and how these patterns affect emotions and behaviors, they can begin to break the cycle of negative and illogical thinking.

Social competence is a complex and difficult construct to assess in adults. A few standardized assessment instruments are available, but many of them have only been used for research purposes (Attwood, 2003) or are only designed for children. Some examples are the Social Responsiveness Scale questionnaire (Constantino et al., 2003) and the Reading the Mind in the Eyes Test (Baron-Cohen, 2004a). The Social Responsiveness Scale provides information on an individual's social behavior as seen from the viewpoint of a parent, caregiver, or spouse. This is valuable because many individuals with social learning disorders cannot really assess their own sociability in relation to the normative population. The Reading the Mind in the Eyes Test is widely used to assess an individual's ability to detect emotional states when looking at eyes.

When selecting participants for the social skills program, a comprehensive clinical interview with the participant and a family member should be used to evaluate the participant's social functioning and to confirm a diagnosis of a social learning disorder. In addition, the participants should complete measures of empathy and sociability using the Empathy Quotient and Friendship Questionnaire (Baron-Cohen & Wheelwright, 2003, 2004) to provide a baseline measure of their social behavior prior to involvement in the course. Furthermore, the parents should complete the Social Responsiveness Scale (Constantino et al., 2003), which provides the family's perspective on the social functioning of the participant. The participants should also complete the Autistic Spectrum Disorders in Adults Screening Questionnaire (Nylander & Gillberg, 2001) or the Autism Spectrum Quotient (AQ; Baron-Cohen, 2004a) to look at specific characteristics that may cause social difficulties, such as a tendency to monopolize conversations or a dislike of spontaneity. The Interpersonal Perception Task-15 (IPT-15; Costanzo & Archer, 1993), which measures the ability to perceive interpersonal dynamics, may also be used for assessment purposes. These measures will provide some information on how the participant perceives and processes the social world.

Many characteristics of adults with social learning disorders are considered in the design of this curriculum. The curriculum provides practical information that is relevant to today's society. It presents information in a straightforward manner that is not ambiguous or subject to misinterpretation. All materials are provided in a written form and are verbally presented. Because processing impairments are common for individuals with social learning disorders, materials avoid idiomatic or metaphoric language. Also, guidelines for behavior are clear and concise. Participants may not want to read lengthy articles and thus prefer summaries instead, such as the handout for Emotional Expression (see Chapter 4), which summarizes Ekman's major themes regarding emotional expression. Web site references are also helpful.

People who have social learning disorders, particularly those with Asperger syndrome, want to know the *why*s of human social behavior. They may not automatically know what to do in social situations, so providing a reason as to why they should maintain eye contact or smile is helpful. For example, if an individual with a social learning disorder knows that the human brain prefers happy faces, and thus more easily recognizes people with happy expressions, the individual may better understand the importance of smiling (Goleman, 2006). The nonverbal aspects of flirtation (e.g., a woman's hair toss, a man's chest thrust) that have been studied by anthropologists and social psychologists can be made more comprehensible by comparing them to mating rituals seen in animals. Therefore, this program draws from a variety of disciplines such as anthropology, neurobiology, and social psychology to explain social behavior.

Program Structure

This social skills program typically is taught over a 12-week period, meeting once a week for a 3-hour session. This structure can be adjusted based on the participants' abilities to sustain attention. Normally the classes have hourly breaks; however, individuals with ASDs may need more frequent breaks, so this should be factored into the class structure. The first 2 hours consist of classroom instruction, whereas the third hour focuses on individualized work with assigned social coaches. Class size is small (8–10 participants) to provide a less intimidating atmosphere for participants, in which they can easily learn each other's names and faces. Classes include men and women, and the instructor should always have an assistant of the opposite sex to maintain a balanced gender perspective on social issues.

Expectations

Class members are expected to be active participants. Consequently, they should not bring hand-held games, laptop computers, or reading material to class. Mobile phones should be turned off during class, as they are often distracting and allow participants to disengage from the class discussion or activity.

Constellation

Participants may be apprehensive about being in a group setting. Some individuals may have difficulty remembering even a few names (or faces) and may be unable to process information from many sources. Others may need encouragement to come at least one time to get a feel for the class. In almost every instance, the participants will be less anxious after the initial class and will be willing to continue. They will meet peers to whom they can naturally relate and will sense a supportive atmosphere. Before class, there may even be a lively conversation occurring among the students, perhaps on the topics of animation, history, video games, or computers.

The participants should have similar educational levels (e.g., high school, college, college bound). Most of the written materials used in the class require a sixth-grade reading level. Although the participants will typically have average to above-average intelligence, they may have learning disorders in the area of language processing. To account for these processing issues, the instructor should frequently rephrase verbal comments and encourage the participants to ask for clarification when needed.

Individuals who have a dual diagnosis with personality disorders (other than schizoid personality) or ongoing substance abuse are not ideal candidates for the program. These issues will be a distraction and require other types of intervention.

Participants should be relatively close in age to address particular developmental stages, such as young adulthood or middle age. The social coaches should also be close in age to the participants to provide a peer relationship. The coaches in the program should be selected based on maturity, commitment, and previous experience. Often, they are graduate students in medicine, psychology, or social work. Each coach should participate in a training session, which provides a background in social learning disorders that is discussed in Chapter 3 and provided in the Social Coach Training slides on the accompanying CD-ROM. However, much of what the coaches learn will be during the class sessions as they establish a relationship with the participant and decide how to best meet that person's social needs. Often, questions will arise and there will be a need for clarification. For this reason, the coaches should continue to receive supervision during the class sessions. New coaches can be paired with more seasoned coaches, who can provide this type of support.

The learning objectives for the coaches' training sessions include the following:

1. Understand the unique social demands of adulthood (e.g., employment, independent living, development of interpersonal relationships)

2. Identify characteristics of individuals with social learning disorders that affect social competency (e.g., theory of mind impairments, communication difficulties, sensory issues, language processing difficulties, cognitive rigidity, poor self-image, social anxiety)

3. Understand the relationship of imitation, mirror neurons, and shared experiences to the development of empathy and perspective taking

4. Understand the value of observation, role playing, and experience when teaching social skills to adults with social learning disorders based on social cognition research

5. Recognize the need to emphasize nonverbal communication and awareness of facial expressions to adults with social learning disorders

6. Recognize the role of cognitive rigidity and executive functioning impairments in social problem solving for adults with social learning disorders

7. Understand the importance of providing explicit social guidelines for adults with social learning disorders

8. Increase awareness of cognitive behavioral techniques to replace negative thoughts about social situations

9. Understand how previous life experiences (e.g., bullying, repeated social rejection) shape the negative self-image and self-defeating behaviors of many adults with social learning disorders

10. Understand the coach's role as a social role model and peer mentor and learn how to set parameters for the coaching relationship

Environment

The classroom environment should be free from sensory distractions such as noise, harsh lighting, or excessive visual stimuli. It is recommended that the classroom have a one-way mirror or videotaping capability, which allows participants and peers to review their classes and instructors to review and monitor exercises. It is important to maintain a supportive atmosphere in the classroom so that participants will feel free to discuss social difficulties and practice in front of each other with the one-way mirror. The instructor should emphasize positive feedback to build a rapport and reshape the negative self-images of the participants. It may be necessary to take short breaks during the classroom portion to provide time for information processing. A combined visual and oral presentation of materials is most effective.

PowerPoint Slides

The accompanying CD-ROM provides PowerPoint slides with visual examples of many of the concepts taught. They provide a sequential format to the instructional portion of the class:

Classes 1–3: Nonverbal communication

Classes 4–5: Conversation skills

Classes 7–9: Interpersonal relationships

Classes 11–12: Career/job interviewing

3

Socializing with Support

Using Social Coaches

> Social skills might be best under-
> stood as access and navigation
> skills . . . they are how we acquire
> desirables and avoid negatives by
> successfully navigating (and mani-
> pulating) the world around us. They
> are complex, multilayered skills
> that are bound by both content
> and context.
>
> Peter Gerhardt (2008)

Social coaches provide the experiential opportunities to produce improved generalization of skills as well as individualized feedback and support. They initiate the practice activities and provide a social role model. In addition, coaches create a feeling of peer acceptance, which is a critical element in improving self-esteem in this population.

Prior to the implementation of coaches in this program in 2005, participants were given homework to reinforce the skills discussed in class. Activities such as initiating conversations and observing nonverbal communication occurred outside the classroom. However, many of the participants were unable to complete these assignments for various reasons. Some participants had difficulty with initiation and tended to avoid the discomfort of a social interaction. Other participants were very fearful of any social activity and needed support to reduce their anxiety. For these individuals, the class was not effective in providing the generalization of skills to the outside world.

To solve these problems, the program looked to the social coaching model (Oden & Asher, 1977) that had been used with children and adolescents in a school setting. This intervention uses direct individual instruction in social skills. The peer mentoring model (McGee, Almeida, Sulzer-Azaroff, & Feldman, 1992) and the peer buddy model (see Copeland et al., 2004; Hughes et al., 2000) have been used to facilitate social interaction in school settings between typically developing children and students with and without disabilities. Therefore, the social learning disorder program decided to recruit coaches who were peers (e.g., similar in age, life stage) of the class participants.

Selection of Coaches

Potential coaches are not difficult to locate in a university environment. Graduate students in psychology, social work, education, and medicine often express interest in the program. Most colleges and university departments have electronic mailing lists of students; initial recruitment of potential coaches can occur through online postings. The screening process should be done by personal interview. Personal qualities of integrity, maturity, and commitment to the program are essential when selecting individuals for social coaching. Some of the coaches may have previous experience working with children or adults with ASDs or other developmental disabilities. These volunteers often want to expand their knowledge of social learning disorders and gain experience working on an individual basis with this population. Many of the coaches may be pursuing careers in medicine, special education, or psychology and welcome the opportunity to get hands-on experience. They can usually use the hours they volunteer to the program to fulfill externship or practicum requirements. All of the coaches selected should be relatively close in age to the participants to serve as peer mentors.

It is important for the coach to have a nonjudgmental and supportive attitude. Most participants will not have previously experienced a feeling of peer acceptance, so the coaching relationship can be helpful in improving their self-esteem. The coaches should be instructed in techniques to reduce anxiety and develop a positive rapport with the participants. All of the coaches should receive a training session on social learning disorders (see the Social Coach Training slides on the accompanying CD-ROM) and 3 hours of continuing supervision as a group.

Being a Social Coach

The role of social coach requires a personal commitment of patience, perseverance, and time. Coaches should be encouraged to attend the social skills class on a regular basis to become familiar with the skills taught, as well as with the participant they are assigned to coach. Coaches who invest this time will find that they have more insights into the social needs of their participants. It is also important that the coaches define the coaching relationship with the participant and set parameters as necessary. Female coaches may work with male participants and vice versa, which could be problematic if the professional nature of the relationship is not defined. For example, one participant tested this parameter by inviting his female coach out to dinner. She responded by informing him that their relationship was a helping relationship, not a personal relationship. He accepted this and was able to benefit from seeing her as a resource to better understand and relate to female peers.

Coaches may be asked to accompany the participants on outings, such as to a restaurant or music club, on their own time. They also should attend the end-of-program party and bring friends for the participants to interact with. One young man who attended this party as a friend of a coach commented that he had difficulty determining who was a participant and who was a coach because the participants were blending in so well.

The Importance of Reliability

Individuals who are chosen as social coaches should be reliable in their attendance to classes and outside activities. Many people with social learning disorders have had very negative experiences with their peers not being reliable or rejecting them by failing to show up for planned social activities. As a result of their negative social history, participants may interpret the unreliable attendance of a social coach as a form of rejection. This hypersensitivity requires that coaches be committed to the program and make every effort to attend. When illness or other reasonable exceptions occur, the coach should contact the participant (by e-mail or telephone) and explain the circumstances. If possible, it is best to make the student aware in advance if time conflicts exist so that the student can be paired with another coach temporarily. Most coaches do not realize how important the coaching relationship is to their student. This relationship may be one of the few positive experiences that a participant has with a peer and therefore it is highly valued. Social coaches are the key element in the program's success.

Individualized Instruction

Because social coaches work on a one-to-one basis with participants, they are able to tailor their instruction to meet the specific needs of the participant to whom they are assigned. At the beginning of the coaching relationship, participants should develop individual social goals with their coaches. The goals can be specific (e.g., improving eye contact) or general (e.g., decreasing social anxiety). The goal should be mutually agreed upon, and it is important that participants identify their areas of need. It is usually advisable to begin working on smaller behaviors and then move to more difficult situations. For example, a participant working on social anxiety may begin by learning to tolerate being in groups of people before moving on to conversation. Participants must learn to stop their avoidance behaviors before any other type of progress is possible.

At times, a coach may use relaxation techniques or guided imagery with the individual before engaging in a social exercise to produce feelings of calm and reduce negative self-talk. The coach's approach must be positive and express hope to combat the internalized negative self-image of many of the participants. Coaches have used exercises from *The Shyness and Social Anxiety Workbook* (Antony & Swinson, 2000b) to address participants' social fears and negative predictions. In particular, it is helpful to identify situations that trigger fearful thoughts. These thoughts (e.g., "People will think I'm nervous") can be challenged with countering strategies (e.g., "What is the worst that can happen?"). These types of questions illustrate that even if these beliefs are true, they are manageable (Antony & Swinson, 2000b).

Changes in social behavior can only be brought about through repeated social exposure. The social coaches are motivators who take the initiative when their participants are struggling. Sometimes it is necessary to model a behavior (e.g., initiating a conversation with a stranger) during an exercise before the participant can follow through.

Training Social Coaches

The Social Coach Training slides (see accompanying CD-ROM) includes a quote from Sean Barron, an individual with Asperger syndrome, who emphasizes the importance of letting go of past negative social experiences in order to be open to establishing new social relationships. This quote is a reminder that people with social learning disorders have to work to become free of their pasts and the unhappy memories that are often revived when they encounter similar social situations. They are often stuck in negative behavioral loops and the associated feelings of failure and low self-esteem.

The opening slides list characteristics of individuals with social learning disorders and the effects of social learning disorders on the quality of life. Knowledge of characteristics such as negative bias and mindblindness are essential in learning to work effectively with participants. Most participants will exhibit some of these characteristics in their approach to learning new social behaviors. Coaches must be prepared to deal with issues such as rigidity and slow rate of processing when working with their assigned participants. It is also important to recognize the life experiences that many participants bring to class, including social isolation, dependency, and mistrust because of bullying by their peers. The coaches must understand the negative mind-set that many of the participants have entering the program.

The next slides present the demographics of past participants and discuss the development of the class over time. The program has added more hours to adequately cover the topics and has used several types of outcome measures to explore the class effect on students' motivation to socialize (Friendship Questionnaire), ability for perspective-taking (Empathy Quotient), and level of social anxiety (Social Interaction Anxiety Scale). The philosophy underlying the development of the program is described by the following ideas:

1. Social behavior can be learned.

2. Experiential activities are the keys to generalization.

3. Individuals with social learning disorders need explicit social guidelines.

4. CBT is used to modify negative bias.

5. Many individuals with social learning disorders need intellectually stimulating materials.

Next, the research on mirror neurons and its theorized relation to the development of empathy is briefly mentioned. The neuroscientist Ramachandran (2000) said that mirror neurons promise to do for neuroscience what DNA did for biology. It is a widely held belief that this groundbreaking discovery is the basis for most human (and primate) social behavior and was essential to the "great leap forward in human evolution" (Ramachandran, 2000). The theory of mirror neurons provides an explanation for complex forms of human interaction and helps us to understand the intentions of others (Iacoboni, 2009). This is the reason for the program's emphasis on role playing and observation to strengthen social cognition and help participants develop the ability to understand other people's actions and mental states.

The goals of social coaching are described in the next slide. The social coaches are providing the missing component of many social skills training programs: facilitated practice of skills and a chance for experiential learning. The role of the social coach is to encourage, guide, and act as a role model for age-appropriate social behavior. Coaching provides an opportunity to tailor skill development to the varying needs of individual participants. The coaching relationship is important to many participants, who feel peer acceptance and improved self-esteem during the course of the program. Coaches also help to calm participants during exercises and are a source of support during more difficult exercises or community experiences (e.g., approaching a stranger to initiate conversation). It is a highly significant relationship for many participants. Therefore, the coach must strive to be nonjudgmental, consistent, reliable, and professional in demeanor.

The components of social awareness proposed by Grandin and Barron (2005) are presented next. Improved self-esteem and social motivation are the main goals of the 12-week course; other aspects of social awareness (e.g., perspective taking, flexible thinking) may take much longer to improve. For some participants, perspective taking will remain very difficult. The goal is for the participant to develop awareness that other people have different experiences of situations and different emotional states as a result.

The next slide provides examples of measurement tools to assess social skill levels prior to and after the course. The Social Responsiveness Scale requires a family member or parent to provide a third-party assessment of a participant's social behavior and therefore involves contacting family members. The Interpersonal Perception Task-15 is used in the first class to provide a quick assessment of the class level of social perception and is then used as a teaching tool.

The 12-week curriculum topics are presented next. Coaches should familiarize themselves with the sequence of the course, which builds upon those topics covered previously. Coaches are also asked to read the article *Better Strangers* (Ramsay et al., 2005) to understand how cognitive behavior techniques are used to reshape negative thoughts and how some of these techniques can be applied to the coaching relationship.

The final slides provide examples of social coaching activities that may be done in class or during the social coaching period at the final hour of class. These examples provide an overview of how the coaching activities reinforce skills learned in class and provide opportunities for self-exploration by participants (e.g., generating an interests list with the coach).

Evaluation of Coaches by Participants

Participants are asked to evaluate their coaches after the 12-week program, using a form loosely based on the California Psychotherapy Alliance Scales (Gaston & Marmar, 1994), a measure used for therapist evaluation (see the Coaches Evaluation handout that follows). The participants should consistently rate their coaches highly in the areas of respect and acceptance, understanding, and dedication to the program. An initial evaluation of the impact of social coaches revealed that participants reported an increase in motivation to socialize, as well as increased social activities at the end of the program, as a direct result of contact with social coaches (Cohen, Rostain, Brodkin, & Sankoorikal, 2006).

Coaches Evaluation

Directions: Below is a list of questions that describes attitudes a person might have about his or her social coach. Think about the course you just completed. Circle the number indicating the degree to which each question best describes your experience.

		Not at all	Somewhat	Moderately	Often	Very much
1.	Did you find yourself tempted to stop an activity when you were upset or frustrated?	1	2	3	4	5
2.	Did you feel pressured by your coach to make changes before you were ready?	1	2	3	4	5
3.	When your social coach commented about one situation, did it bring to mind other related situations in your life?	1	2	3	4	5
4.	Did you feel that even if you might have moments of doubt or confusion, overall the experience was worthwhile?	1	2	3	4	5
5.	Did your social coach's comments lead you to believe that your social coach placed his or her needs before your own?	1	2	3	4	5
6.	When important things came to mind, how often did you find you kept them to yourself rather than sharing them with your social coach?	1	2	3	4	5
7.	Did you feel accepted and respected by your social coach for who you are?	1	2	3	4	5
8.	Did you find your social coach's comments unhelpful, confusing, mistaken, or not really applying to you?	1	2	3	4	5
9.	Did you feel that you were working together with with your social coach to overcome your problems?	1	2	3	4	5
10.	How free were you to discuss personal matters that you are ordinarily ashamed to reveal?	1	2	3	4	5
11.	During this course, how dedicated was your social coach to helping you overcome your difficulties?	1	2	3	4	5
12.	Did you feel that your social coach understood what you hoped to get out of the course?	1	2	3	4	5
13.	Did you feel you were working at cross purposes with your social coach or that you did not share the same sense of how to proceed so that you could get the help you want?	1	2	3	4	5

Source: Gaston & Marmar (1994).

(continued)

Coaches Evaluation *(continued)*

14.	Did you have the impression that you were unable to deepen your understanding of your social difficulties?	1	2	3	4	5
15.	How much did you disagree with your social coach about what issues were most important to work on during this course?	1	2	3	4	5
16.	How much did your social coach help you gain a deeper understanding of your social difficulties?	1	2	3	4	5

Source: Gaston & Marmar (1994).

4

Understanding Nonverbal Communication

With most people, the nonverbal communication supplements or enhances the verbal communication. The two channels are processed together to give a deeper meaning to the communication. With people having autism or Asperger syndrome, however, the nonverbal component can be so difficult to decode that it interferes with getting meaning from the verbal channel. As a result, very little, if any, communication occurs.

Stephen Shore (2001)

It is estimated that 80%–90% of our communication is nonverbal (Givens, 2011), involving body posture, gestures or facial expressions, or paralanguage (i.e., vocal features that accompany speech–e.g., loudness, tempo). Nonverbal communication includes all human communication other than words themselves. Teaching adults with social learning disorders to recognize nonverbal communication is fundamental to their understanding of social behavior. Although most individuals with social learning disorders know that making eye contact is considered important, they frequently find it awkward and distracting. For these individuals, processing visual information and verbal information simultaneously is difficult. Often, as they are concentrating on verbal processing, they neglect the nonverbal information that is present in a social encounter. Even when they learn to make eye contact with other people, they may not read the nonverbal information presented in facial expressions and other forms of body language, perhaps because of social anxiety or the inability to process verbal and nonverbal cues simultaneously. This difficulty interferes with every aspect of their social awareness because the integration of verbal and nonverbal information is the essence of social communication.

Assessment of Nonverbal Decoding Skills

To assess an individual's ability to decode nonverbal cues, visual material, such as video vignettes or muted scenes from movies, may be presented. To focus on nonverbal cues, brief scenes from movies can be shown and participants asked about their perceptions of what was happening in each scene. The idea was derived from a study in which individuals with high-functioning ASDs watched scenes from *Who's Afraid of Virginia Woolf?* without sound while researchers recorded their eye gaze patterns (Klin, Jones, Schultz, Volkmar, & Cohen, 2002). The researchers found that subjects' eyes often looked at the background rather than the characters' faces. Golan, Baron-Cohen, and Hill (2006) have also used scenes from films to assess social understanding in the Reading the Mind in Film task. The subjects were asked to select an adjective from four choices to describe the way the character feels at the end of the scene (Golan & Baron-Cohen, 2006).

When doing this exercise in the social skills program (see Exercise 1, in Class 2), the movies used should be from the drama or thriller genres, which tend to draw viewers' attention to the characters' facial expressions. Older films are preferred, such as Alfred Hitchcock movies or film noir, because the participants may be less familiar with them and the techniques used for dramatic effect often involve prolonged camera shots of faces. The selected scenes should be 5–7 minutes long and focus on only a few characters. Movies with large ensemble casts are too difficult to follow and provide too much distraction for this type of exercise. Some television comedy shows such as *The Office*, *30 Rock*, and *The Big Bang Theory* use exaggerated facial expressions for comedic effect and also work well. Many participants in the program have said that the Japanese style of animation seen in graphic novels (manga) and movies (anime) are preferred because the facial expressions are drawn larger and more exaggerated, which aids in their understanding of the characters' emotions.

Although many of the participants may enjoy fantasy and science fiction movies, these genres should not be used in the exercise because they do not provide the real-life interactions that participants must confront in their everyday lives. Scenes involving male–female relationships are particularly valuable to illustrate the nonverbal aspects of attraction, flirtation, and also rejection. These are especially challenging for adults with social learning disorders, who frequently misinterpret the other person's intentions. It is also valuable to analyze scenes to determine the perceptions of the interpersonal dynamics.

Another way to assess nonverbal communication skills is the Interpersonal Perception Task-15 (IPT-15) developed by Berkeley Media (Costanzo & Archer, 1993). This video presents a series of 15 short scenes, after which the viewer is asked to answer questions based on his or her perception of what was communicated verbally as well as nonverbally. The interactions represent status, deception, kinship, intimacy, and competition. The task is challenging and requires concentration. Although the IPT-15 is complex and at times frustrating, it most closely resembles real-life interactions in which simultaneous processing of verbal and nonverbal cues is required. This video can be used for assessment and as a teaching tool. The scenes can be reviewed many times to provide practice in detecting the more subtle gestures that may be overlooked initially.

Teaching Recognition of Facial Emotions

Darwin was the first to study and catalog human emotional expression (Keltner, 2009). He created very detailed descriptions of emotional expression in humans by studying photographs of actors portraying different emotions and also wrote about emotional displays in animals. Darwin posited that the human ability to recognize emotions in others and respond in kind has evolved and is strengthened by habit and social practice. Contrary to the idea that humans are aggressive and violent by nature, Darwin argued that the ability of humans to empathize and care for others is the critical element in their survival as a species (Keltner, 2009).

There is a large body of research on human facial expressions, much of which has been carried out by Dr. Paul Ekman. In his book *Emotions Revealed*, Ekman (2003) explored the universality of human facial expressions and the core emotional expressions of happiness, sadness, disgust, anger, contempt, fear, and surprise (see Handout 1 at the end of the chapter). Emotional expression is not a learned behavior and is universal from culture to culture as a result of our social evolution. Primates express anger by baring their teeth in preparation to bite. This behavior is also seen when humans express extreme anger, as well as in milder expressions of anger that involve a clenching of teeth. Chimpanzees express disappointment with lips pursed just as humans do (Holmes, 2008).

Dawn Prince-Hughes, an anthropologist with Asperger syndrome, learned from her study of gorillas how to interact socially with people. She wrote,

> The gorillas had an enormously calming effect on me. They knew and recognized me, briefly acknowledging my presence each time I sat with them. But their behavior was subtle. . . . Their social subtleties and calm demeanor allowed me to relax and really watch what they were doing. I saw social cause and effect for the first time. When I realized that their behavior was so much like human behavior I knew I would learn everything I needed to know from them. (2002, p. 117)

Prince-Hughes applied the behaviors that she learned from the gorillas (e.g., making people feel relaxed by sitting near them and smiling) to her own social situations. For example, Prince-Hughes determined that "smiles evolved from submissive primate grimaces and mean that the person intends no harm" (2002, p. 117). She also learned that primate gestures (e.g., putting up your hands and lowering your head to avoid an argument) translated well to the nonverbal communication seen in humans.

Although facial expression of these core emotions is universal, people differ from culture to culture in what is taught about managing or controlling facial expression of emotion. Research conducted by Ekman (2003) examined these cultural differences. A stress-inducing film was shown to both American and Japanese college students. When the students were watching the film alone, they had virtually identical facial expressions, but when they watched with another person present, there was a difference: The Japanese students masked their facial expressions of unpleasant feelings more than the Americans. This cultural difference is a result of the display rules learned in Japanese culture that emotional expression in public is undignified.

To teach recognition of facial expression of the core emotions, the Micro Expression Training Tool (METT) developed by Ekman and Friesen (2003) can be used. This software is designed to teach individuals how to recognize brief expressions of emotion by learning what areas of the face are involved in each expression. For example, the expression of disgust involves the center of the face and a wrinkling of the nose. These expressions are only shown for a fraction of a second, requiring quick observation of the key elements of the face. Most emotional expression is very fleeting (2–3 seconds), but the METT focuses on emerging emotions and provides even more fleeting images. If the participant learns to quickly recognize these expressions, he or she will be able to identify longer emotional displays in real-life situations.

The Subtle Expression Training Tool (SETT) (Ekman, 2009) can be used to teach subtle expressions of emotion such as mild anger. These are the types of information that adults with social learning disorders typically miss. These individuals are often able to read facial expressions, but they do not always attend to the face during an interaction. These exercises reinforce the importance of looking at someone directly. Both the SETT and METT are available for purchase at http://www.paulekman.com.

With a team of scientists, Dr. Simon Baron-Cohen developed the *Mind Reading Emotions Library* (2004b), which teaches a wide variety of facial expressions. The expressions are grouped by categories, such as hurt expressions, excited expressions, unfriendly expressions, or romantic expressions. There are many examples in each category. The actors performing the different expressions represent a wide range of ages and are both male and female.

Humans automatically mimic behavior. This mimicry facilitates social understanding and interpersonal rapport. In one study, individuals with ASDs did not automatically mimic the emotional facial expressions of others when shown pictures of faces that were happy or angry. However, they were able to imitate the expression when asked to (McIntosh, Reichmann-Decker, Winkielman, & Wilbarger, 2006).

Typically, individuals experience activation of the mirror circuit when viewing others' facial expressions (Carr, Iacoboni, Dubeau, Mazziotta, & Lenzi, 2003). Individuals with ASDs, however, seem to have an impairment of a basic automatic social-emotion process (McIntosh et al., 2006). Compensatory strategies, such as the mirroring technique discussed in the next section, may help these individuals to become more automatic in the imitation of facial expressions.

Mirroring to Reinforce Nonverbal Awareness

Social psychology research indicates that subtle imitation of another's body language, facial expression, and voice tone creates a feeling of bonding. The mirroring technique causes the other person to feel more relaxed and connected to you. It is often used by salespeople and others who want to create a feeling of trust (Peterson, 2005). Feeling in sync with another person often heightens rapport. In his book *Social Intelligence*, Daniel Goleman (2006, p. 31) states "the more two people unconsciously synchronize their movements and mannerisms during their interaction, the more positively they will feel about their encounter—and each other."

Mirroring, also known as *parallel body language*, is a good exercise for observing nonverbal cues. Participants in the social skills program should practice mirroring (see Exercise 2, in Class 2) to have a greater awareness of nonverbal communication, as well as to experience feelings of attunement with their partners. Although forced mimicry of another person seems mechanical at first, it can gradually become a complementary rhythm. Social behavior that feels positive has "an elegant orchestration of movement, turn-taking, and gazes" (Goleman, 2006, p. 31) and is often referred to as a social dance.

Components of Nonverbal Communication

According to researchers Eryilmaz and Darn (2005), nonverbal communication—just like any language—has form, function, and meaning. The components of nonverbal communication include the following:

1. *Kinesics (body language):* Body motions, such as foot tapping and shrugs; eye movements, such as winking, facial expressions, and gestures
2. *Proxemics (proximity):* Use of space to signal privacy or attraction
3. *Haptics:* Touch
4. *Oculistics:* Eye contact
5. *Chromatics:* Use of time, waiting, pausing
6. *Olfactics:* Smell
7. *Vocalics:* Tone of voice, timbre, volume, speed
8. *Sound symbols:* Grunting, "uh-huh," mumbling
9. *Silence:* Pausing, waiting, secrecy

10. *Posture:* Position of body, stance

11. *Adornment:* Clothing, jewelry, hairstyle

12. *Locomotion:* Walking, running, staggering, limping

Most of the focus will be on increasing awareness of eye contact, facial expressions, gestures, proximity, posture, voice tone, and volume. Exercise 2 allows participants to practice both observing and imitating these nonverbal forms of communication. It is very effective to videotape these exercises to provide visual feedback of the nonverbal signals the participants are sending. Often, participants are not aware that their voice is too soft or too loud, their posture is poor, or their proximity is too distant until they see themselves on video.

Another resource for nonverbal information is *The Nonverbal Dictionary of Gestures, Signs and Body Language Cues* (Givens, 2011). This dictionary provides information about nonverbal communication from the perspectives of archeologists, anthropologists, biologists, linguists, neurologists, psychiatrists, and psychologists. It covers gestures such as arm crossing, shoulder shrugging, hands on hips, and specific facial expressions and their meanings. For example, touching one's lips is a self-consoling gesture that diverts attention from disturbing thoughts or people. This gesture may signal anxiety, excitement, fear, or uncertainty. From a neurological perspective, touching the fingers to the lips is a form of acupressure.

This type of reasoning for a particular behavior or action can be presented to more highly educated participants. These individuals are often interested in the scientific explanations for social behaviors, which seem to demystify the otherwise confusing rituals of social interaction. This may be particularly true for the topics of physical attraction, courtship, and dating (see Chapter 6).

Practicing Nonverbal Observation Skills

The use of social coaches provides opportunities to practice skills outside the classroom (see Exercise 3, in Class 2). Participants should be asked to visit public places (e.g., a train station, restaurant, bookstore) with their coaches to observe people. They should be directed to distance themselves so they are not close enough to hear dialogue but can only observe nonverbal behaviors. After the observation, they can discuss their impressions of the people based on only the nonverbal cues. Then they are asked to predict what might happen next.

The participants may create scenarios about those they observed. This exercise can help them to start analyzing situations prior to their own actions. For example, they may read the body language of a group of people before deciding to join them. Their nonverbal cues would indicate whether they are open (looking outward) or closed to accepting a new person. Many participants report feeling rejected in party situations when, in reality, they may not be making a good decision about whom to approach based on nonverbal cues. Ekroth (2004) advises readers to "prequalify" people who might want to converse. Usually these people are looking around the room or scanning for an opening. This type of exercise is also very helpful in understanding how the participants interpret nonverbal behavior. It is important that participants evaluate the body language of anyone whom they might approach. They should avoid people who are engaged in other activities or look preoccupied. Social coaches can help them to determine (based on nonverbal cues) who looks open to converse.

Misinterpretation

Although many participants miss important nonverbal cues, they sometimes infer too much from the nonverbal behavior they observe and make broad assumptions accordingly. Assertions such as, "He looks like he's cheating on his wife," are illustrative of this type of inference. It is not possible to infer this from a limited nonverbal observation; however, participants may sometimes make these kinds of judgments. The nonverbal behavior may signal a discomfort or secrecy, but one cannot infer an extramarital affair.

This tendency to overinterpret may be the result of limited experience or may be related to a desire to simplify a very complex set of stimuli. Many individuals with social learning disorders engage in black-and-white thinking. That is, as a result of their inability to understand the complexity of human behavior, they characterize people as either good or bad. In reality, a person's social behavior is complex and has both positive and negative aspects.

Faulty attributions made by participants are illustrative of the kind of misperceptions that create problems in their everyday interactions. Research has shown that people with social learning disorders often do not see the big picture. Instead, they are caught up in details and do not integrate the totality of the experience. This analysis of the interaction as a whole is crucial to formulating an appropriate response. It is always important to examine the perception of an individual with a social learning disorder because it may be very different from the reality of a situation.

Analyzing Nonverbal Cues Before Initiating Contact

An important aspect of understanding nonverbal communication is using the cues to determine whether a person may be receptive to interacting. If someone is reading, listening to music on headphones, or otherwise occupied, that person is usually not receptive to engaging in conversation. A person usually indicates that he or she is open to interaction by body stance and eye contact. If a person is facing you and looking out in your direction, that body language suggests that the person may be receptive to conversation. In a party atmosphere, people often scan the room with their eyes when looking for someone to talk with. If someone's back is turned away and there is no eye contact, this body language suggests a lack of interest. These distinctions often elude individuals with social learning disorders. They do not recognize nonverbal cues, which minimizes their probability of success when initiating a conversation.

Class 1: Introduction

The objectives of Class 1 are to

- Introduce class members
- Review course description and syllabus
- Collect baseline data using the Social Interaction Anxiety Scale (Mattick & Clarke, 1998)
- Evaluate nonverbal communication awareness using the Interpersonal Perception Task-15 (IPT-15; Costanzo & Archer, 1993)
- Complete the Social Activities Scale with coaches

Introduction of Class Members

The class members should take turns introducing themselves briefly (one or two sentences). Always ask each class member to mention a personal area of interest. This is important because there is usually at least one other classmate with a similar interest (e.g., music, computer games, animation) and this can facilitate conversation among class members, as well as increase their feelings of comfort and acceptance.

Course Description and Syllabus Review

The class is designed to teach a broad range of social skills and increase feelings of social competence. The 12-week class syllabus, which may outline the classes and their objectives, should be reviewed with participants to give an overview of the course and explain the role of coaching activities. It should be explained that some of the topics covered may seem very basic, but the goal is to increase class members' understanding of social behavior, which is often subtle and indirect. All class members will build on their existing strengths and not focus on their weaknesses. The importance of practicing the skills outside of class as well as with the coaches should be stressed. On the accompanying CD-ROM, slides are included to aid in the presentation of background and overview information in this program.

Baseline Data Collection

To provide outcome measures of class effectiveness, two self-report instruments at the first and last class should be administered. This usually takes about 20 minutes of class time. The Friendship Questionnaire (Baron-Cohen & Wheelwright, 2003) measures interest in people and motivation to socialize. The Social Interaction Anxiety Scale (Mattick & Clarke, 1998) evaluates fear of social situations.

Evaluate Nonverbal Awareness (Interpersonal Perception Task-15)

The Interpersonal Perception Task-15 (IPT-15; Costanzo & Archer, 1993) is an interactive exercise that is a good method for obtaining baseline data, as well as for use as a teaching tool to introduce the importance of nonverbal communication. As discussed previously, the IPT-15 is a video containing 15 brief scenes. The participants are given answer sheets (which are included with the video) prior to the exercise. There is a question presented before each scene (e.g., "Who is the child of the two adults?") and then the scene plays. The viewer must attempt to answer the question by decoding nonverbal cues (e.g., voice tone, body proximity, gestures) or at times by the dialogue cues. The vignettes depict common types of social judgments regarding kinship, intimacy, status, competition, and deception. This task is difficult, and this should be explained to the participants beforehand so they will not be overwhelmed. It is a valuable tool because it approximates real-life situations. After the exercise is completed, the scenes are replayed and the explanations for the correct answers are discussed. The administration and follow-up discussion usually lasts over an hour. The IPT-15 can be purchased from http://www.berkeleymedia.com.

Social Activities Scale with Coaches

Each participant is assigned an individual coach to work with during the 12-week course. Participants and coaches should spend a few minutes getting to know each other after the initial introduction. Coaches may exchange e-mail addresses with their participants so they can maintain contact outside of class. The participants and coaches should then complete the Social Activities Scale together (see Handout 2 at the end of the chapter). This activity facilitates discussion of the participant's current level of social activity and also helps the coach to determine realistic short-term goals for increasing social activity. It is important for coaches to recognize that a reasonable socializing goal may be quite less than their own level of socialization.

Class 2: Mirror Neurons and Nonverbal Communication

The objectives of Class 2 are to

■ Increase nonverbal awareness (Exercise 1)

■ Understand the concept of mirroring (Exercise 2)

■ Understand the different types of nonverbal communication

■ Observe examples of nonverbal communication (Exercise 3)

Increase Nonverbal Awareness

The focus of Class 2 is to provide participants with a variety of opportunities for observing and imitating others' nonverbal behaviors. To create an opportunity to view body language, short movie clips can be shown without sound. The participants should determine the emotional feeling of the scene and the relationships among the characters based solely on nonverbal cues. Older movies provide slower pace and longer camera shots of facial expressions and are therefore preferred. Television dramas and comedies can also be used for this exercise (Exercise 1). The participants should write down their impressions of what is happening in the scene and then a class discussion should follow. Some suggestions of films are *All About Eve, Chocolat, The Talented Mr Ripley, Shadow of a Doubt, Dial M for Murder,* and *Five Easy Pieces.*

■ **Exercise 1.** Nonverbal Observation

You will be asked to watch a short video clip without any sound. The only information you will have about the scene will be from the nonverbal cues you are able to pick up from the characters. After viewing the video clip, please answer the following questions.

1. What is your overall impression of what was happening in the scene?

2. What emotions did you detect in each of the characters? What nonverbal cues (body language, gestures, facial expressions) did you detect that created your impressions?

3. What is the relationship of each of the characters to the others?

4. What is the emotional tone of this scene?

5. What might happen next?

Understand the Concept of Mirroring

Social psychology indicates that subtle imitation of another's body language, facial expression, and voice tone creates a feeling of bonding between two people. This technique is called mirroring. People use the mirroring technique to create a more relaxed and connected feeling, which is also called attunement. It is important to emphasize to the class that mirroring should be subtle in order to be effective. In this exercise (Exercise 2), class members are paired and each should observe the actions of the other person to whom they are speaking. The observer attempts to incorporate the voice tone, posture, and hand gestures of the other person. The exercise continues as the partners trade places of who is the observer and who is the imitator. This exercise can be done in front of a one-way mirror so the rest of the class can observe. Another option is to videotape the mirroring exercise and then let the class watch each pair. Hand mirrors can also work as an option in class to allow the participants to observe their own facial expressions such as sadness, anger, or surprise. Mirroring creates an opportunity for class members to observe their own body language as well as the body language of others.

Exercise 2. Mirroring

Social psychology research indicates that subtle imitation of another's body language, facial expression, and voice tone creates a feeling of bonding (Goleman, 2006). This mirroring technique causes the other person to feel more relaxed and connected to you. It is often used by salespeople and others who want to create a feeling of trust. Mirroring also provides good opportunities to observe nonverbal cues.

While having a 5-minute conversation about a recent trip or outing you took, have one person mirror the other's nonverbal signals. Then switch roles and let the other person do the mirroring.

Observe Examples of Nonverbal Communication

Many people with social learning disorders do not pay attention to body language. They must acquire information about body language by learning to observe others. The social coaching activity in Exercise 3 is used to increase awareness of other people's nonverbal communication. Class participants should repeat these types of exercises independently during the week so they have many opportunities to observe nonverbal behaviors in different settings.

Exercise 3. Social Coaching

Observe people in a public space such as a coffee bar, restaurant, train station, shopping mall, or park. Position yourself at a distance so you cannot hear them but can only watch their body movements, gestures, and facial expressions. Be discreet and do not stare. Try to focus on interactions between people—specifically, their nonverbal behavior in relationship to each other.

Were the interactions positive, negative, or neutral? List examples on a separate sheet of paper.

Class 3: Facial Expressions and Cues

The objectives of Class 3 are to

- Become familiar with core emotions
- Recognize facial expressions using the Mico-Expression Training Tool (METT; Ekman & Friesen, 2003)
- Understand subtle expression of emotion using the Subtle Expression Training Tool (SETT; Ekman, 2009)

Recognize Facial Expressions/Core Emotions

Class 3 entirely focuses on one realm of nonverbal communication: the recognition of human facial expressions. Drawing from the work of Dr. Paul Ekman, the class explores the expression of the seven core emotions (happiness, sadness, disgust, anger, contempt, fear, surprise). The class uses the METT, which teaches individuals how to recognize brief expressions of emotion by learning what areas of the face are involved, as discussed previously. An alternative to using the software is to use the pictures in the back of *Unmasking the Face* (Ekman & Friesen, 2003). Also, the *Mind Reading Emotions Library* (Baron-Cohen, 2004b) teaches a wide variety of facial expressions. There are 24 emotion groups represented, as well as vocal recordings of these emotions. The emotions are grouped into six different levels of difficulty, so the software can be used by children as well as adults. It is available for purchase through Jessica Kingsley Publishers (http://www.jkp.com).

It is important that participants are able to identify basic emotions that they will encounter in real-life situations. The slides on the accompanying CD-ROM also provide a charades exercise to give the participants opportunities to practice different types of body language (both facial expression and gestures). A hand mirror is helpful for participants to see their own facial expression of these emotions. Another possible activity is to view a clip from the Fox television show *Lie To Me,* which is inspired by a real-life specialist who "reads" expressions, body language, and voice to help solve criminal investigations (Fox, n.d). This show often uses Dr. Ekman's research.

Understand the Subtle Expression of Emotion

Emotions such as anger are often repressed. Therefore, it is critical to learn the subtle signs of this emotion. The software programs SETT and Emotions Library, as well as the exercises in *Unmasking the Face,* point out the subtle changes involved in emotions such as sadness, happiness, surprise, and fear, which have a range of expression. Contempt and disgust are fairly straightforward emotions that do not have the same degree of subtle expression and are usually easy to distinguish. All of these exercises reinforce the importance of looking at someone during a social interaction. Although human emotions are universal, the expression is usually culturally determined. Handout 1 summarizes Dr. Ekman's findings about expression of emotions across cultures. It is important to stress that culture often plays a role in emotional expression. For example, European and Middle Eastern men may kiss each other as a greeting, and Middle Eastern men may often hold hands. This type of nonverbal gesture of affection is rarely seen among heterosexual men in the United States; instead, handshakes are the norm. Asian cultures stress emotional restraint in public settings and not touching one another when greeting friends or acquaintances, whereas Mediterranean cultures tend to be quite open.

Handout 1: Emotional Expression

Emotional expressions are universal; however, different cultures have "display rules" for managing expressions.

Facial expressions are innate, not learned.

Basic facial expressions are fear, surprise, anger, disgust, contempt, happiness, and sadness.

Subtle expressions are weak/diminished emotions or suppressed emotions.

It is best not to comment on subtle emotions noted in another person unless you know the person very well.

Emotional awareness takes time to develop as a skill; after continued practice, the eye becomes educated.

Emotions are often brief, lasting only a few seconds.

If an emotion lasts for hours, it is called a mood.

People experience emotions as happening to them, not as chosen by them.

Displays of emotion are involuntary and hard to fake.

Emotions bind people to one another.

Source: Ekman (2003).

Handout 2: Social Activities Scale

Please indicate how often you have engaged in the following activities over the past month.

1. Made a phone call for social or friendship reasons

2. Answered the phone without letting it go over to voice mail

3. Went out to a group activity

4. Went to a party

5. Went out to the mall, bookstore, and so forth

6. Went to a movie, concert, or show

7. Went out with a friend

8. Made a new acquaintance

9. Made contact with someone you are interested in dating

10. Went out on a date with someone

11. Sent someone a personal e-mail

12. Had a conversation online with someone you are interested in dating

Source: Rostain, Cohen, & Brodkin (2003).

5

Improving Conversation Skills

By its very nature, small talk will not always thrill or delight. Knowing this ahead of time will greatly reduce the chances of the Aspie saying something a bit too bold like "Don't you have anything interesting to talk about?"

Liane Willey (2001)

A few of the participants in the social skills seminars may be reserved, but many of the individuals with Asperger syndrome will be quite verbose. However, despite their comfort with words, most of these individuals do not know how to initiate or sustain a conversation. Their style is to monologue rather than dialogue. Small talk, which is required in initial social interaction, is irritating and pointless from their perspective. They often may not understand the concept of reciprocity in communication and tend to monopolize the conversation. Consequently, the other party may feel offended and walk away in the middle of the discourse. Individuals with social learning disorders, who are rigid in their behavioral repertoire, may continually repeat this mistake with countless other people but not understand why they get the same reaction.

Conversations have a natural progression. The interaction normally becomes more significant and meaningful as it proceeds through four levels: clichés (small talk), facts, opinions, and feelings (Garner, 1997). Often the purpose of small talk is to provide an initial exchange of niceties before getting to the "meat" of the conversation. In other instances, such as social gatherings, small talk is the primary form of exchange.

Because most of the program participants want to have more in-depth discussions, they often ignore the role of small talk as an icebreaker. They want to skip this progression and begin talking about complex topics from the start. An example of this occurred once when participants were practicing conversation skills behind a one-way mirror. One participant immediately started talking about his study of certain philosophers. Using no icebreaker topics such as the weather, sports, or a current event, he launched into a philosophical discourse that many people would find intimidating and uninteresting.

45

Teaching the Art of Conversation

As this social skills seminar developed, social skills coaches developed an exercise to improve small-talk skills that is based on the concept of speed dating. The coaches should have participants engage in five 3-minute conversations (15 minutes total) with different people by moving from table to table. The idea is to simulate the number of short exchanges one might have at a party and become familiar with the "small talk script."

In addition to getting accustomed to small talk, it is important that people with social learning disorders become familiar with how a conversation progresses. They may not feel comfortable with self-disclosure of information or they may self-disclose too early in the interaction. Either way, their participation in a conversation is hampered. They must learn that self-disclosure is usually "symmetrical," with people sharing information about themselves at the same rate. Self-disclosure of information keeps conversations going through asking questions and finding similarities or links to one's own experiences (Garner, 1997).

Another issue in conversation is learning the social "rhythm"—when to enter or interject comments, not monopolizing, and how to recognize when the other person is becoming disinterested. These skills can be practiced with the social coach, who should provide feedback on the conversational flow.

It is often helpful to have participants generate possible topics before actually initiating a conversation. This is also a good strategy for conversing on the phone. The speaker can have the list of topics in front of him to ease anxiety and create a structure to the verbal exchange. Small talk does not come easily to these individuals. Therefore, any strategy to create a sense of structure will reduce their tension. Many individuals with social learning disorders report that they freeze up during casual exchanges because they do not know what to say next. Repeated practice with a coach helps to desensitize them and rehearse for future encounters.

Because of their lack of social awareness, individuals with social learning disorders may introduce topics that can cause problems. For example, during casual encounters with strangers or acquaintances, many participants have expressed political views or other opinions that are likely to be off-putting. They may also introduce highly personal information that can make the other party uncomfortable. Some of these errors are related to their lack of ability for perspective taking. To avoid these pitfalls, the program includes some general guidelines for casual conversations (see Class 5 on the accompanying CD-ROM).

Another challenge that many people with social difficulties face is remembering names. It is common not to be aware of other participants' names after several classes even though the class is small (6–8 participants). The importance of using a person's name when having a conversation should be emphasized. It elicits participants' attention and makes them feel recognized. Also, this is a method for reinforcing the name in memory. This technique, combined with sustained eye contact, can create a feeling of connection between the speakers.

Another strategy that can be taught is to make a diagram of an office or classroom where the participant encounters people on a frequent basis, with the seats or offices labeled with the appropriate names. This technique was used by a law student with Asperger syndrome who could not remember the names of classmates. Because the law students had assigned seats, the participant was able to start remembering names as the students were called on by the professor. For some participants, it is also helpful to write down a few additional descriptive details about the person (e.g., brunette, tall, wears glasses). Some participants have also stated that they cannot recognize voices of people they know on the phone. As a result, they avoid answering the phone or making calls. Use of caller identification is recommended for landline phones, and most cellular phones can identify the caller from a directory created by the user.

Evaluating Body Language

Using a one-way mirror or videotaping conversations in class provides important information about the participants' body language. Most of the participants report that watching themselves is very helpful. They may be unaware of their posture, their voice volume, or how they hold their head when engaging in conversation. Many participants who are socially anxious look down when they are talking and avoid eye contact. This posture also causes their voice to project downward, which makes it difficult to hear what they are saying. In contrast, some of the more gregarious participants with Asperger syndrome talk too loudly.

To evaluate these nonverbal aspects of communication, a rating scale is used (see the Conversation Skills Rating material at the end of this chapter and the Class 5 slides on the accompanying CD-ROM). The Conversation Skills Rating covers nonverbal conversation skills such as eye contact, body posture, and proximity, as well as voice tone, volume, and inflection.

Eye contact skills include having a soft expression in the eyes, as opposed to a hard stare, and taking brief intermittent breaks from eye contact. Many individuals with social learning disorders have been told to constantly make eye contact; as a result, it looks as if they are staring at the other speaker. This creates discomfort for the other party and is also difficult to maintain. It is natural for the eye to take intermittent breaks from looking at the other person. These breaks are fleeting (1–2 seconds) and expected by the other party.

Body proximity is also important in conveying a feeling of connection. Standing or sitting at a distance that is too great creates the impression that the speaker is aloof. A comfortable distance for standing is usually an arm's length from the other person. When seated, chairs may be at a greater distance, but the speaker can lean forward to convey interest. A person who sits with his or her back straight against the chair also creates an impression of aloofness. A person with an open posture (i.e., arms relaxed at side, legs open) looks more approachable than one with crossed arms and legs.

Many of the participants may have difficulty looking relaxed while being attentive to another person. Often they may need to loosen their posture before beginning a conversation. They should lean forward and not have a stiff back while seated. They should keep their head level to project their voice outward instead of downward. Also, participants should be encouraged to keep their hands and legs open (not crossed) to reduce physical tension.

Evaluating Conversation Skills

When rating the overall quality of the conversation, the Conversation Skills Rating focuses on five areas: opening, closing, topic, topic transitions, and balance between speakers.

The opening should consist of a greeting (and handshake if appropriate). The closing is just a quick comment that politely denotes the end of the conversation, such as "It's been nice talking to you." These types of structured exchange are often neglected by adults with social learning disorders, who start talking about a topic without exchanging a greeting or abruptly end a conversation.

The issue of topics is also very important in creating a comfortable conversation. Highly charged social or political issues of the day (e.g., abortion, gay marriage, terrorism) often make others uncomfortable in casual conversation. The program encourages participants to stay with neutral topics that are not as emotionally charged. Also, it is important to stick to topics that have mutual interest. For example, if one of the parties indicates that he does not like baseball, it would be inappropriate to continue talking about the subject at length. Many individuals with social learning disorders do not understand the concept of mutual interest because they are so intensely interested in certain topics themselves. It is difficult for them to understand that others do not share their enthusiasm for video games, Japanese animation, or Russian history.

Topic transition should be smooth. This is done by using connecting phrases such as "speaking of sports" or "on the subject of movies." These types of phrases prepare the other party for an upcoming transition. Although many of the participants will be very verbal, they may bombard people with a lot of random information. It is important to stress the need for topic transition to create coherence. Often, participants may be so engrossed in a particular subject that they jump from one idea to another and leave the other party confused.

It is very helpful to videotape conversations to provide examples of these issues. When the participants watch themselves on video, they can see how the conversation progresses and concentrate on the mechanics.

Conversational balance between the speakers is evaluated by how long each party is speaking. To create balance, the participants should be encouraged to ask open-ended questions or make comments that require more than a *yes* or *no* response (e.g., "What about the movie did you like?" "Tell me more about your hometown"). Another way to draw the other person into the conversation is to ask *you* questions rather than just making *I* statements. That is, instead of taking the conversation back by talking about themselves, participants should ask questions such as, "What did you think of the book?" These techniques create more opportunity for dialogue and produce more interesting exchanges. The idea of reciprocity is also to seek a balanced exchange in the course of a conversation. If a speaker introduces a topic and the other person has no response, it is time to move to another topic of mutual interest. The analogy of a tennis game may be useful to illustrate conversational balance: A question is lobbed to one speaker, who then returns with a response and another question.

Listening skills may also be an area of difficulty for many people with social learning disorders. When participants are not interested in what the other person is talking about, they may stop listening or interrupt in a blunt manner. Being a polite and active listener requires nonverbal behaviors such as eye contact, leaning in, and nodding the head. It is also important to clarify what the other person is saying by echoing a key word or phrase used. Another way to indicate interest is by probing with phrases such as, "Tell me more about that" (Horn, 1997).

Class 4: Conversation Skills, Conversation Progression, and Small Talk

The objectives of Class 4 are to

- Understand barriers to conversation
- Understand conversation progression
- Recognize the importance of small talk
- Recognize the importance of listening skills
- Learn ways to initiate conversation

Understand Barriers to Conversation

Class 4 explores the basic skills of conversation. Many individuals with social learning disorders do not know how to initiate or sustain a conversation. To improve their conversation skills, it is imperative that they understand the concept of reciprocity or conversational balance. The most common problem for individuals with Asperger syndrome is that they monopolize the conversation on their topic of interest, never asking questions of the other party. Many are experts on their topic of interest, which leaves little opportunity for the other person to contribute. A conversation must have a give-and-take quality where all parties feel that they are giving and receiving information. A good conversation feels balanced, with each person feeling he or she had an opportunity to contribute. Most good conversations leave each party feeling that he or she came away knowing the other person a little more.

Understand Conversation Progression

Conversations have a logical progression from small talk to more significant or meaningful topics. It is a common mistake of individuals with social learning disorders to avoid small talk and launch directly into a highly charged discussion of a topic of interest (e.g., politics). This is overwhelming to the other party, who was probably expecting some icebreaker conversation to occur. Although conversations about opinions and feelings are generally more interesting, these types of topics can be introduced comfortably only after some basic information has been exchanged. Although it is certainly desirable to disclose some information in an initial meeting (e.g., where one lives, works, or goes to school), it is inappropriate to disclose personal information (e.g., medical problems, traumatic events, family history) in a first-time meeting. After getting to know an individual, self-disclosure of personal experiences is natural; however, it should be symmetrical, with each party disclosing information about him- or herself at the same rate.

Recognize the Importance of Small Talk

Many people with social learning disorders consider small talk to be boring and unnecessary. However, it is a social prerequisite to more significant interaction and exists in all cultures. Small talk is often the primary form of exchange at social gatherings. Discussion of opinions and feeling too early in the conversation will tend to make other people feel uncomfortable, particularly if during a first encounter. The sequence of conversation is important to give each party a feeling of getting to know the other before the topics progress to more significance. The logical progression of most conversations (e.g., small talk, facts, opinions, feelings) is explained in Handout 3.

Recognize the Importance of Listening Skills

One exercise that can improve listening skills is to have each participant tell a quick anecdote at the beginning of class. After a short break, ask one specific detail about each of the anecdotes to see how well the class was listening. Often, people with social learning disorders will focus on what they are going to say next and will not fully listen to the person with whom they are speaking. This type of exercise can improve concentration and shift focus to what others are communicating.

Anyone who wants to be a good conversationalist will first have to learn to become a good listener. Effective listening is active rather than passive. The art of listening involves certain body language that denotes interest in what is being said. First, listeners should position themselves to face the speaker and slightly incline their bodies toward the speaker. Listeners should also maintain an appropriate distance (a few feet or arm's length) and maintain an open position (arms uncrossed). It is important to maintain eye contact with the speaker using a relaxed gaze (soft eyes) rather than an intense stare. While listening, it is important to register interest by nodding the head, making short verbal comments (e.g., "yes," "uh-huh"), and showing interested facial expression (not blank looks). Listening is respectful of others and makes them feel that what they are saying is interesting. Even if someone is not that interested in what the other person is saying, it is important not to interrupt or appear bored. There will always be an opportunity to change the topic later. Handout 4 summarizes these points about effective listening and starting conversations.

Initiate Conversation

Starting a conversation can be as simple as asking whether someone has read a particular book (e.g., "I'm looking for a summer read. Have you read this?") or even offering a compliment ("I really like your necklace. Is it handmade?"). Conversations can be initiated this way or at a social gathering by introducing yourself and then asking a question (e.g., "Are you a freshman?"). Open-ended questions will elicit more conversation because they cannot be answered with a simple *yes* or *no*. Open-ended questions usually start with phrases such as "Tell me about . . . " and require a more in-depth response.

Common Interests

It is best to ask others about their interests and then see if there are any common areas of interest to talk about. People respond positively when questions are asked that show the other party is interested in them. It is flattering and creates a good feeling in them. The opposite is true when the conversation is one-sided and only one person talks about himself.

Social Coaching Activity: Starting a Conversation

The coach and participant should go to a busy bookstore and observe the people there. The participant should identify (with help from the coach) someone who looks "open" to conversation based on his or her body language. The coach should stand off to the side while the participant approaches the person. The participant should ask the person for a book recommendation as a means of starting a brief conversation. If the person does not respond positively or seems too busy to talk, then the participant should just move on politely. It is important to point out that people who are reading, wearing headphones, or using a laptop are not good candidates for conversation. If the person does respond, the participant may continue the conversation by asking a few other questions (e.g., "What authors do you enjoy?"). The participants are usually nervous before engaging in conversation and need the coach's support to help relax them. They may be anticipating a negative outcome and need some positive thoughts before they initiate the conversation. The coach can also give some suggestions for how to keep the conversation going and can intervene if the participant is talking too long. Afterward, social coaches will provide feedback about participants' conversation skills (using the Conversation Skills Rating). This exercise helps to reduce anxiety about talking to strangers and can greatly improve self-esteem.

Class 5: Self-Disclosure, Problematic Topics, and Social Rhythm

The objectives of Class 5 are to

■ Practice conversation skills
■ Evaluate conversations using the Conversation Skills Rating

Practice Conversation Skills

The focus of this class is to have the participants practice conversations with different partners and then be rated using the Conversation Skills Rating (Handout 5). Each participant practices a 5-minute conversation with different partners behind the one-way mirror so the class can observe. The following prompt is used: *A new neighbor has just moved into your neighborhood and this person just knocked on your door.* The participants take turns being the new neighbor so everyone gets to play each role. Conversations usually center on what the neighborhood has to offer (e.g., recreation, entertainment, restaurants) but can cover a number of topics.

Evaluate Conversations Using the Conversation Skills Rating

The class observes the conversation through the one-way mirror (or by video recording) and then rates the two speakers on core conversation skills outlined on the Conversation Skills Rating. The rating evaluates five areas of conversation: opening, closing, topics, topic transition, and balance between the speakers. The class gives the two participants verbal feedback about the conversation specific to the scale (e.g., "Your posture indicated interest because you were leaning toward them"). It is important to focus on each partner's positive behaviors first. This kind of feedback is helpful in improving the participant's skills but should never be overly negative.

Conversational Flow

The slides on the accompanying CD-ROM (see Class 5) provide an explanation of *social rhythm,* which refers to keeping a conversation flowing by not interrupting or monopolizing, and monitoring the other person's interest level. Strategies for conversations are provided in Handout 6. The slides also review the body language components for conversations (e.g., body proximity, eye contact, open posture) that are to be rated. Many individuals with social learning disorders do not understand body proximity. They may stand too close or too far away from the other speaker. Often in group situations, the individual may stand on the periphery of the group, so that the group members are not aware that the individual wants to be included in the conversation.

Social Coaching Activity: Speed Conversations

Divide all participants and coaches into conversation partners (using chairs facing one another) and practice having an initial "getting to know you" conversation for 3 minutes. At the end of that time period, rotate to another conversation partner and continue at 3-minute intervals until everyone has had a conversation with everyone in the room. This exercise is also a good preparation before the end-of-class party because it has similar social demands to a party atmosphere where conversations are brief (Dokun & Rostain, personal communication, July 23, 2007).

Class 6: Outing with Social Coaches

The objectives of Class 6 are to

- Increase comfort with social interaction
- Improve conversation skills
- Generalize skills

At this point in the course, it is customary to have an outing with coaches. The class has just finished conversation skills, so this gives them an opportunity to practice conversation skills with other members of the class and other coaches. The purpose of this off-site meeting is to build upon the previous classes and activities. Participants get the opportunity to practice skills learned and observed and develop social relationships with others in the class. Usually this outing is a dinner at a nearby restaurant, but it can also be an activity like bowling or miniature golf. When going to a restaurant, it is important to request tables that are close to each other to facilitate interaction among the various class members. Long rectangular tables are not preferable because it is too difficult to talk with other members. Round tables with chairs or booths create a good atmosphere for discussion. The class usually chooses a restaurant that is acceptable to everyone, taking into consideration food preferences, dietary issues (e.g. vegetarian, Kosher), and cost. Class participants are not allowed to bring any items that will distract them from having a conversation (e.g., handheld games, books, iPods), and cell phones are kept "at bay." Class participants are encouraged to talk with as many people as they can. Many individuals with social learning disorders are not familiar with this kind of social interaction. The coaches will need to prompt them and give them suggestions about topics they can bring up for discussion.

Handout 3: Conversational Progression

1. Small talk, clichés

"How are you?"
"How's it going?"
"What's new?"
"How do you like this weather?"
"What did you think of last night's game?"

These ritual openings are not designed to discuss anything of substance. They serve as ice-breakers. As in many social behaviors, small talk is a means for each person to become accustomed to the other.

2. Facts

"I live in Philadelphia."
"I'm a software designer."
"I'm going to Boston for two weeks' training."
"I like to jog three times a week."

After exchanging small talk, people usually proceed to exchanging facts. In early exchanges each person tries to find out if there is enough to share to make a relationship worthwhile.

3. Opinions

"I prefer living in a small town where I know everybody."
"I want to date a lot before I get serious about anybody."

Opinions give others a more personal view of you. If you express them in an open-minded way, your opinions can provide others with material on which to base interesting conversation.

4. Feelings

"I felt angry and frustrated when Jake got hired instead of me."
"I'm really pleased with the way I was welcomed into the neighborhood. It made me feel good."

Feelings convey your emotional reaction to a situation or event. Expressions of feeling give closer insight into who you are.

Source: Garner (1997).

Handout 4: Conversational Skills

Effective listening

1. Incline your body toward the speaker.

2. Position yourself to face the speaker's face (be at eye level).

3. Maintain an open position (arms and legs uncrossed).

4. Position yourself at an appropriate distance from the speaker (a few feet if seated; an arm's distance if standing).

5. Focus your eyes softly on the speaker and occasionally shift your gaze (do not stare blankly or look away from the speaker).

6. Register interest by facial expression, nodding, or verbal comments.

Starting conversations

1. Ask questions that deal with the other person's interests.

2. Ask open-ended questions about the person's job, school, and so forth.

3. Give a compliment (only to a person of the same gender).

4. Mention a current movie, television show, or book.

Handout 5: Conversation Skills Rating

1	3	5
Poor	*Fair*	*Good*

Eye contact

Overall _____

Soft eyes _____

Intermittent breaks _____

Body posture

Overall _____

Head and shoulders _____

Leaning forward _____

Arm/hand position _____

Leg position _____

Voice

Volume _____

Tone _____

Intonation _____

Conversation

Closing _____

Describe the overall quality of the interaction from your perspective and what you think each speaker was feeling during the interaction:

Handout 6: Conversation Strategies

1. *Make eye contact with the person speaking.* People like you to look at them. It indicates you are interested in them and that you are paying attention.

2. *Use the person's name when speaking to them.* People like to be called by name. It is more personal and indicates that you are interested in them.

3. *Stay on topic.* Changing topics can confuse the other person. Indicate when you are changing the subject by using a transitional phrase.

4. *Use body language to indicate you are interested.* Facial expressions and nodding show that you are listening and responding to what is being said. Leaning toward the speaker also indicates interest.

5. *Notice the other person's facial expressions.* Be aware of other people's expressions while you are talking. They may indicate that they are enjoying, bored by, or even upset by what you are saying.

6. *Avoid personal or controversial topics.* Do not discuss sensitive topics such as politics, religion, or personal issues with people you do not know well.

7. *Ask questions of the other person occasionally.* Asking questions allows the other person to participate in the conversation and also indicates that you are interested in his or her experiences, views, and ideas.

8. *Avoid using offensive language.* Try to avoid using offensive words or terms or language that may be derogatory. Some people are offended more easily than others so it is better to err on the side of caution.

6

Interpersonal Relationships and Dating

> An ability to let go of the past has gotten much easier as my range of experiences has grown. The more situations I live through, the better able I am to put them into perspective and let those that are inconsequential fall by the wayside. The more I connect with people—my family, friends, coworkers, even strangers—the greater appreciation I have for each person who is in my life.
>
> Sean Barron (as cited in Grandin & Barron, 2005)

A common misconception about individuals with social learning disorders is that they are loners by choice. In reality, most adults with social learning disorders are interested in having relationships but do not understand friendship or sexual/romantic relationships. They are often extremely lonely and searching for human connection. Dr. Tony Attwood (2009) reported that the most predictive research variable of positive quality of life for adults with Asperger syndrome is the amount of hours spent with friends—the greater the hours, the more positive their perceptions of life satisfaction.

The approach to relationships taken by adults with social learning disorders tends to be either too intense or too detached. Their limited emotional knowledge results in an often childish approach to adult relationships. They are often not able to distinguish friends from acquaintances or love from social attraction (Berney, 2004). These factors complicate the already complex issue of teaching relationship skills.

Family Relationships

Many people with social learning disorders have experienced repeated rejections from the opposite sex. As a result, they may have a negative self-concept and expect to be rejected in social encounters. A lowered head, looking down at the floor, and rarely making eye contact are not characteristics that attract others. Such body language projects a negative image, which leads to more rejection from the outside world. This vicious cycle is repeated until the person decides to retreat from all social contact.

Many individuals with social learning disorders have given up on the idea of ever being able to socialize, so they tend to isolate themselves at home. This creates a great deal of stress for their families, who are often their only social outlet. Siblings often bear the brunt of this responsibility (Willey, 2001). Siblings may try to include the individual with a social learning disorder when they are with friends, but this often leads to resentment. In addition, the individual with a social learning disorder becomes dependent on siblings to provide a social life and does not initiate any social contacts of his or her own.

Relationships with parents are often stressed due to the increased dependency and reliance of the individuals with social learning disorders on parents for total support. Many parents may feel trapped in a situation of providing for the needs of their adult child while at the same time encouraging more independent functioning. This is complicated by the fact that many individuals with social learning disorders do not drive and are dependent on parents and other family members for transportation. The parents may have very protective instincts for their adult child from years of witnessing their child being socially rejected by others. These parents have good intentions but have difficulty allowing their adult child to have the experiences (positive or negative) necessary for social awareness and growth. If parents are always available for outside activities (e.g., movies, bowling, sporting events), an adult with a social learning disorder will not learn to take the initiative to create his or her own social life.

Parents are often advised to "pull back" their involvement in their adult child's life but continue to provide structure and support. An individual with social learning disorder may have difficulty with independent functioning and may need a gradual approach. Having their own apartment may be overwhelming to many individuals with social learning disorders, but living with a relative can be a first step to increased independence. There are many options for people with additional support needs, such as finding a roommate with similar needs and hiring a social coach or vocational-rehabilitation counselor to be in regular contact with them.

Dr. Digby Tantam (2005) has suggested that many people with social disorders are marginalized by being overindulged by their families. The family members have great empathy for the person with a social learning disorder, but often ignore the individual's uncaring and exploitative behavior. Many families allow individuals with social learning disorders to control all family activities (including mealtimes) around their own idiosyncratic schedules. This further confuses individuals with social learning disorders, who may not understand the social consequences of this behavior in the outside world. Consequently, when they engage in selfish and thoughtless behaviors outside of the home, they only experience more social rejection and isolation (Tantam, 2005).

Friendships

Friendship skills are "the foundation of abilities that are highly valued by adults in their professional and personal lives, namely having teamwork skills, the ability to manage conflict and having successful personal relationships" (Attwood, 2009). Most individuals with social learning disorders desire friendships but lack the necessary understanding of what is required to establish and maintain friendships.

Young children with ASDs should learn what it means to have a friend (Attwood, 2009). Often these children consider anyone in their class or a next-door neighbor a "friend," regardless of whether they have any social contact with that person. This immature concept of friendship does not evolve as in a typical child's development. Instead children with ASDs must be taught "friendship skills" such as reciprocity, assistance, initiation, and conflict resolution.

Because adults with social learning disorders have minimal experience with friendships, they often do not truly appreciate the concept of friendship. They perceive anyone who is nice to them as a friend but do not understand what constitutes a true friend. Their desire for relationships often sets them up to be used by unscrupulous individuals. The naiveté of adults with social learning disorders makes them an easy mark for those who are manipulative and want something from them. Many of these individuals report being used for money or favors, such as one young man who drove 3 hours to pick up an item for a "friend" and never heard from the person again.

These types of experiences may cause anxiety about any new relationship and often cause individuals with social learning disorders to avoid people in general.

Connecting with Like-Minded Individuals

It is important to recognize that most relationships revolve around shared interests and activities. For participants, that interest could be music, art, computer games, or Japanese animation. The key to developing relationships is to find places where people with these similar interests gather and then to join them. Participants should be encouraged to join computer gaming clubs or go to cartooning conventions, film festivals, or any other place where people have interests similar to theirs. Finding these kinds of connections is the first step to decreasing their sense of isolation. Participants will discover that there are many people with whom they can share their consuming interests. These specific interests can be the basis for romantic relationships as well. Participants can use the Internet (e.g., http://www.meetup.com) to find groups for a variety of different interests.

Many adults with social learning disorders may attempt to use interactive social networking sites (e.g., Facebook, MySpace, Twitter), e-mail, and online chat rooms as a source of outside contact but rarely ever initiate any face-to-face meetings. Adults with social learning disorders often resign themselves to fantasy Internet relationships to allay their intense loneliness. However, their reliance on computers as a safe way to meet people does not reduce their anxiety about socializing. For example, they may try to accumulate a large number of online contacts but never have any relationships beyond e-mail. One participant reported that he had several hundred people on his Facebook friend list but did not really know any of them. These superficial relationships do not help the individual with social learning disorder learn lasting interpersonal skills. Although it can be enjoyable to establish online relationships, participants should be encouraged to take the next step of developing social relationships, which involves face-to-face interactions.

The lack of boundaries in the Internet world often makes it a dangerous place for those with social learning disorders. They often lack social awareness and an understanding of what is appropriate to share on the Internet. Many of these individuals may reveal highly personal details or even discuss sensitive family issues online. One young man was surprised at the negative reaction he received after posting personal details about his classmates on a web site.

Flirting

Understanding courtship displays and attraction signals is essential in the world of dating. Many of these behaviors are nonverbal and subtle, which can be difficult for individuals with social learning disorders to interpret. Flirting is mainly nonverbal and involves having an open body position, raising the eyebrows to express interest, tilting the head and exposing the neck in women, sustaining eye contact, leaning forward, and glancing sideways then shyly smiling (Luscombe, 2008). Many participants may be totally unaware when someone is flirting with them. These individuals often miss subtle behaviors—both flirtation and friendly gestures—and consequently miss the opportunity to respond to them. One young man was so focused on getting to his classes on time that he would not notice people saying hello along the way. It was as if he had social blinders on that prevented him seeing anyone on the periphery. Other students thus perceived him as aloof or as avoiding them.

Dating

Most people find dating to be an awkward but necessary ritual. It is a way to meet potential love interests. Individuals with social learning disorders find the ritual of dating particularly stressful because of their low self-esteem and fear of rejection. Jerry Newport, who is diagnosed with Asperger syndrome, wrote that many people with ASDs do not date because of their own negative self-images (Newport, 2003). They are highly critical of themselves and do not always see themselves to be worthy of a relationship. These negative perceptions are difficult to change and require patience and an establishment of trust. Indeed, many people with social learning disorders anticipate negative outcomes before they even make contact with someone.

Flirtation, sexual attraction, and romantic interest are complex human behaviors that are often subject to misinterpretation. Sean Barron, an adult with Asperger syndrome, wrote that for years he interpreted a woman initiating a conversation with him as a sign of romantic interest and failed to see any other possible meanings. As a result, he was constantly on an emotional rollercoaster with women, going from "euphoria to heartbreak" (Grandin & Barron, 2005, p. 256). He did not understand that friendliness was not necessarily a sign of romantic attraction—a common problem for many men with social learning disorders. Mainly because of their lack of experience, people with social learning disorders may interpret a compliment or friendly gesture as an indication that others want to date them. These individuals should learn to see a pattern of encouraging behaviors from others before assuming those people are interested in dating.

This program uses a two-strikes rule for asking someone out on a date. If the participant asks someone out on a date and that person declines because he or she is busy, then the participant should only ask one more time. If that person is busy the second time, then the participant should not ask again unless given some specific encouragement.

It is also important for the participant to ask someone out in person or on the phone. Important cues, such as voice inflection, are missed when communicating online. When dealing with dating and romantic relationships, it is important to have as much nonverbal information as possible to determine the emotional state of the other person. Conversations should occur face-to-face, particularly when trying to decipher another's romantic intentions.

Participants are encouraged to watch relationship movies to become more familiar with how attraction is expressed nonverbally. Romantic comedies, such as *When Harry Met Sally*, can provide lots of examples. These films can also be used to explore gender differences in perspective. Female peers may also be invited to class to answer questions about their attitudes about dating. To provide some structure to the concept, dating guidelines that reflect current trends are provided on Handout 9 (see Class 8). These guidelines stress the consideration of the other person's interests and preferences.

Although there are many reputable dating web sites on the Internet, caution must be used when becoming involved in this process. Participants may have unrealistic expectations that they can meet and establish a relationship online without actually dating. Their reliance on the computer as a sole means of social contact perpetuates this belief. Because of their low self-esteem, they do not feel that they can be successful meeting someone in person.

The Internet can be a great resource to connect with people, but it does not help improve social skills beyond this initial online contact. After researching suggestions for Internet dating for people with Asperger syndrome, the guidelines on the accompanying CD-ROM were developed (see Class 8). A helpful resource is the web site Wrong Planet (www.wrongplanet.net), which contains articles on dating and relationships for individuals with Asperger syndrome. Most of the site's content is useful for all people with social learning disorders.

Intimacy and Sexuality

It is a common misconception that individuals with social learning disorders do not desire intimate relationships. Because of their lack of interpersonal relationships, they may not have had the opportunity to experience the intimacy of a best friend or lover. As a consequence, they may not fully understand the concept of intimacy. The sharing and trusting aspects of an intimate relationship may elude them. Intimate relationships are not always sexual relationships. Several components define what makes a relationship intimate:

- A sense of a special bonding
- Sharing of tenderness, caring, and affection
- Sharing of secrets and private thoughts
- Mutual respect
- A sense of being accepted and valued as a person
- A nonabusive, noncoercive relationship

Dr. Isabelle Hénault, a psychologist and sexologist who works with adults and adolescents with ASDs, stated that her clients often engage in risky sexual behavior because they have no concept of what is appropriate. They may not understand what constitutes inappropriate touch or sexual language (Hénault, 2007). An individual with a social learning disorder may not know when it is appropriate to touch someone (whether it be kissing or holding hands) because of their lack of experience and inability to read sexual cues. When trying to create guidelines for this behavior, it is important to focus on the body language of the other person such as proximity, intensity of eye contact, and sexual cues (e.g., self-touching). If other people desire physical contact, many times they will initiate touch by moving closer or intensifying their gaze.

Biology plays a significant role in sexual attraction and how we select a mate. Because of these physiological factors, true chemistry between people can only be determined in face-to-face encounters. For men, sexual attraction is largely visual; for women, it is thought to involve smell (pheromones). Women report being attracted to the smell of their partners (Goleman, 2006). According to Dr. Gordon Gallup, a psychologist who studies sexual attraction, kissing involves "a rich exchange of postural, physical, and chemical information" (Kluger, 2008). In addition, kissing passes testosterone to the woman, which is a natural aphrodisiac.

Class 7: Interpersonal Relationships

The objectives of Class 7 are to

- Recognize characteristics of healthy interpersonal relationships
- Explore Internet relationships
- Understand Internet safety

Recognize Characteristics of Healthy Interpersonal Relationships

Many individuals with social learning disorders have had minimal experience with friendships and do not fully appreciate the concept of friendship. Friendship must be a give-and-take relationship. A relationship without reciprocity is unbalanced and may be unhealthy. Previous negative experiences with other people have caused people with social learning disorders to become mistrustful and avoid relationships in general. These points from *The Unwritten Rules of Social Relationships* help to characterize the important aspects of friendship (Grandin & Barron, 2005, p. 239):

- Friendships take time to develop and require work to maintain.
- People can disagree and still be friends—friends don't have to agree on everything.
- Friends are genuinely concerned about each other's feelings and thoughts.
- Friends help each other out in times of need.
- There are relatively few people who are your really close friends.

Handout 7 summarizes suggestions for initiating friendships and maintaining them. It is important to emphasize that friendship requires flexibility and reciprocity. Many individuals with social learning disorders may wait for others to initiate a social activity. These individuals should start initiating social activity because others may not be aware that they want to socialize, particularly if they have been socially avoidant in the past. To practice, participants can write a script for inviting a specific person to go to the movies. For this class, have the participants bring their cell phones and ask them to call that person during the coaching portion of class. The coaches can help the participants review what they will say prior to the call and provide support.

Explore Internet Relationships

The Internet can be an invaluable tool for initiating social contact. Although it can be enjoyable to establish online relationships, participants should be encouraged to take the next step of having face-to-face interactions. Before making arrangements to meet someone in person, it is important to have a phone conversation. This is a logical progression of social exchange and allows both parties to establish more personal contact. Superficial relationships do not help an individual learn lasting interpersonal skills.

Understand Internet Safety

Although there are many reputable web sites for meeting others, including dating web sites, caution must be used when becoming involved in this process. It is important to be very careful about information posted online. Many web sites do not allow direct exchange of information such as home address or telephone number. These precautions are for personal safety. There are some good web sites for connecting with people with similar interests, such as http://www.meetup.com. This web site provides information for groups of similar interests all across the country; it has been used successfully by many people with social learning disorders for a wide variety of purposes, not just dating.

The Internet can be a great resource to connect with people, but it should never be used as a primary means of social exchange. Social networking sites such as MySpace, Facebook, and Twitter have been shown to increase social behavior overall. However, face-to-face contact is the only way to really improve social skills. Online relationships do not provide the valuable information that hearing a person's voice or observing their body language can provide for determining whether there is a feeling of social connection. Handout 8 lists some suggestions for using Internet dating sites and suggestions for Internet safety. Participants should complete Exercise 4 on writing an Internet dating profile or Facebook page.

Exercise 4. Writing an Internet Dating Profile or Facebook page

1. Using the suggestions from Handout 8, compose a profile that you would submit to an online dating service. Remember to be honest, to be positive, and to emphasize your interests.

2. Create a Facebook page for yourself that describes your personal characteristics (e.g., creativity, humor), interests (e.g., music, cartooning), and what type of activities you enjoy (e.g., movies, bowling, museums). Do not include highly personal information (e.g., your address, your telephone number).

Class 8: Dating

The objectives of Class 8 are to

- Understand the dating difficulties of individuals with social learning disorders
- Understand intimacy
- Review dating suggestions

Understand the Dating Difficulties of Individuals with Social Learning Disorders

Class 8 explores the topic of dating. The following are reasons that people with social learning disorders may find dating and romantic relationships to be particularly difficult:

- They are late bloomers socially.
- They have less social experience than their peers.
- Many have negative early experiences (e.g., bullying).
- Many are distrustful of people.
- They often do not initiate social contact because they fear rejection.
- They often do not follow up to maintain relationships.
- They may spend too much time with their special interests and neglect relationships.
- They find relationships to be complicated and confusing.

The last point should be emphasized because many participants think that everyone else finds this process easy. However, most people recognize that relationships are messy at times and require effort to maintain. This may not be apparent to individuals with social learning disorders, who may instead perceive other people to be more popular, interesting, and desirable.

Understand Intimacy

Because of their lack of interpersonal relationships, many people with social learning disorders have not had opportunities to experience the intimacy of a best friend or lover. Therefore, they may not fully understand the concept of intimacy. Be sure to emphasize that intimate relationships are not always sexual relationships. The following list of characteristics of intimate relationships, previously mentioned in the main chapter text, should be used to engage the class in a discussion about intimacy:

- A sense of a special bonding
- Sharing of tenderness, caring, and affection
- Sharing of secrets and private thoughts
- Mutual respect
- A sense of being accepted and valued as a person
- A nonabusive, noncoercive relationship

An intimate relationship requires time to develop. People who have long-term friendships (often childhood friends) and long-term romantic relationships reach this type of intimacy. These relationships are unique because there is often a "sixth sense" that develops between people where they communicate on a nonverbal level. More information on intimacy in relationships can be found at http://www.coping.org/relations/intimacy.

Review Dating Suggestions

Handout 9 provides dating suggestions designed to give the participants some guidelines. Although there are no rules for dating, there are ways to reduce social anxiety by planning a structured activity and keeping the first date short (under 3 hours). An individual who is feeling nervous can excuse him- or herself and take a short break in the restroom. For a first date, the web site www.wrongplanet.net suggests going to a movie and then going to a coffee shop afterwards to discuss it. The movie provides a topic for conversation, which will reduce the amount of time that the individual has to freely converse.

Social Coaching Activity: Dating Panel

This exercise is designed to give the participants an opportunity to ask the coaches' panel dating and relationship questions. It is important to have both male and female coaches on the panel to provide different gender perspectives on these issues. The participants can ask direct questions about how the coaches would react in certain situations (e.g., "How would you feel if a guy you didn't know well in your accounting class asked you to have dinner with him?"). The coaches should be instructed to not answer highly personal questions or those dealing with their own sexual history.

Class 9: Attraction and Sexuality

The objectives of Class 9 are to

- Understand biological attraction
- Recognize nonverbal aspects of flirting
- Understand healthy sexuality

Understand Biological Attraction

Class 9 explores the biological components of why people are attracted to one another. Much of why people are attracted to a certain type of person depends on factors such as body shape, smell, and even evolution. For example, men tend to prefer women with hourglass figures because, from an evolutionary standpoint, women with large breasts and wide hips are more successful bearing children. Men's brains are imprinted to be more dependent on visual cues for attraction. Women are much more sensitive to smell, which explains why they are more interested in fragrances (e.g., perfume, scented products) than men. There has been research done to explore why women are attracted to men based on olfactory preferences. Scientists have discovered that the scent of a man's perspiration can have major effects on women's moods, causing them to feel happier and more relaxed (Goleman, 2006). Women may even be attracted to men initially almost solely based on smell. In a romantic setting, such as sitting close together or dancing with their bodies close, people respond to these chemical aspects of arousal.

People often comment that the first time they kissed someone, there was a feeling that a mysterious force was pulling them together. Kissing is a biologically driven impulse that is initiated through eye contact. When a couple gazes into each others' eyes, the orbitofrontal areas of the brain are activated, which cause emotions to be aroused and acted upon. Pheromones and physical contact certainly play an important role in feeling romantic about another person. This is why it is important to have close contact with a person (instead of looking at a photograph or talking online) to determine whether this type of chemistry exists. This point should be emphasized many times in the program because many of the participants are socially avoidant. Participants may think that they can meet their true love online and develop a significant romantic relationship before ever meeting them in person. These relationships usually do not work out because all the physical aspects of attraction have been ignored. Handout 10 summarizes some key points about the role of biology in attraction.

Understand Nonverbal Aspects of Flirting

Flirtation is mostly nonverbal and is derived from courtship displays that have evolved over time. Many individuals with social learning disorders do not look at people and therefore are often unaware when someone is flirting with them. They may miss the nonverbal cues of flirtation and not respond, so the other person moves on. Human courtship, as with other animals, follows a predictable sequence: eye contact, smiling, preening, talk, then touch (Pease & Pease, 2001). The eye contact stage is usually initiated by the woman, who will gaze at the man for about 5 seconds and then turn away. This is usually repeated several times. A woman may also look sideways over her shoulder at a man just long enough for him to notice. Next, the woman may smile quickly, which indicates that she would like the man to approach (smiling is always a welcoming signal). The woman usually preens by sitting up straight (emphasizing the breasts) or tilting her head to the side to expose more of the neck. She may also adjust her clothing or jewelry, flick her hair, or lick her lips. The man responds similarly by touching his hair, expanding his chest by standing up straight, or adjusting his clothing. They both point their feet or entire bodies toward each other. Next, the man may approach and initiate small talk (e.g., "Come here often?") just to get the conversation started. The woman may initiate a light touch (e.g., brushing against the man's shoulder) or even touch his hand to indicate she is interested in him. She wants to see his reaction to this and whether he seems comfortable. It is best if the woman is the first to initiate touch. Examples of these types of flirting behaviors (with photographs) are found in the January 28, 2008, *Time Magazine* article entitled "Why We Flirt" (Luscombe, 2008). Watching movies or television shows that deal with relationships and identifying examples of nonverbal flirtation can be a good class exercise to increase this awareness.

Understand Healthy Sexuality

Many people with social learning disorders have had little or no sexual experience in relationships. As a result, they do not always understand what is sexually appropriate. It is not uncommon for individuals with social learning disorders to base their expectations on what they have seen in pornographic or even mainstream movies (which is never or very rarely realistic). These individuals are often intimidated by these expectations because they cannot distinguish the fantasy from reality. These individuals may think that people perform as they do in these fantasy scenarios, which may not show all the emotional aspects of sexual relationships. Individuals with social learning disorders may also be under the misconception that everyone engages in casual sex after a brief encounter, as television shows may skip the relationship and fast-forward to the bedroom scene. Therefore, it is important that participants have an opportunity to discuss realistic views of sexuality and its place in an intimate relationship.

The corresponding slides on the accompanying CD-ROM may generate some questions and discussion in small groups. These topics can be discussed openly (but not graphically) in the seminar. The social coaches should address the participants' questions about the appropriateness of when to initiate sexual touching in a relationship. Most touching has a progression from holding hands to kissing to more intimate physical contact. The guidelines are simply that each person must feel comfortable with physical touching and not be coerced. Sometimes participants are not comfortable with touching and need more time. It is always important to share this information with one's partner. There is nothing offensive about expressing the need for more time; this should not be interpreted as a rejection. There are many different styles and personal preferences when it comes to physical intimacy. There are no set rules for when a couple may choose to become sexually intimate, but it should always be a mutual decision.

Handout 7: Making and Keeping Friends

Take the initiative to reach out to others. Do not wait to introduce yourself, but rather initiate the first activity.

Remember facts and details about other people so they know you are listening and care about what's going on their life.

Don't come on too strong. Be casual, informal, and comfortable. Use small talk first.

Try to meet people with similar interests. For example, you can attend an art class, chess club, or comic convention.

Plan activities around mutual interests.

Be open to new experiences. For example, you can try a new type of food or listen to a new type of music.

Respond to e-mails and telephone calls in a timely fashion.

Reciprocate when someone invites you to do something by suggesting a future outing that you will plan.

Handout 8: Internet Dating Suggestions

- Talk about your likes and dislikes in your personal information. Do not characterize dislikes as complaints.

- Describe your physical features, such as eye and hair color.

- Look for dating sites with easy access and flat-fee structures.

- Use a current photograph that looks like you.

- When you contact someone, do not lead in with a request for a meeting or date.

- Keep your messages short.

- Keep track of your contacts and messages.

- Do not discuss personal subjects or opinions in e-mails.

- Avoid commenting on issues such as age and physical appearance. Some people may be sensitive in these areas.

- After several messages, suggest talking by telephone. This is the natural next step. If you feel comfortable after talking with the person on the telephone, you can suggest meeting in person at a public place, such as a coffee shop.

- When you meet the person, have a friend call your cell phone to check in and make sure you are feeling comfortable. Do not make this obvious to the person you are meeting. It might be helpful to identify a code word to use that indicates you are fine.

Handout 9: Dating Suggestions

Plan the date ahead of time.

Pick an activity that the other person is interested in.

Avoid movies that are violent or overly sexual.

If you are going to a restaurant, ask about food preferences.

If you initiate the date and choose the restaurant or activity, be prepared to pay for both of you.

Keep the first date under 3 hours (even if you are having a good time).

Ask questions about the other person to get to know him or her.

Listen to the other person and show you are interested in what he or she says. Do not talk about yourself too much.

Do not spend a lot of money. Allow the other person to pay if he or she offers.

Do not talk about personal topics (e.g., your parents' divorce) on the first date.

Relax and let the other person get to know you.

Handout 10: Biology of Attraction

- Men are more visually oriented in their initial attraction; the sight of an attractive woman activates the brain's pleasure centers.

- Smell is an important element of initial attraction for women; the scent of a man can cause romantic feelings, calmness, and a sense of security.

- Flirting usually is initiated by the woman with a smile and brief eye contact. The flirter gazes directly at the target and then glances away.

- You must have a face-to-face encounter with someone to know if you are physically attracted to him or her. This cannot be determined just by looking at a photograph.

- Gazing at someone causes our brain to feel linked to the other person and emotionally attuned (this usually occurs before kissing).

Source: Goleman (2006).

7

Employment Issues and Job Interviewing Skills

If I were a computer, I would have a huge hard drive that could hold 10 times as much information as an ordinary computer but my processor chip would be small . . . I cannot do two or three things at once.

Dr. Temple Grandin (1999)

Temple Grandin and other adults with ASDs have emphasized the importance of finding employment that is a good fit for the individual's interests and strengths (Grandin, 1999; Grandin & Duffy, 2004). Unfortunately, some people with social learning disorders were never encouraged to pursue their true interests. Instead, they may have felt pressure to enter fields that are very taxing to their social skills and knowledge of relationships, such as teaching, sales, or customer service. These types of work environments can cause great stress for individuals with social learning disorder because of the constant demands for social interaction and little downtime.

Many people with social learning disorders need to have an environment that is relatively quiet, a place where they can work without interruption, and a job with some solitary time built into the workday (Grandin, 1999). Examples of ideal jobs include computer programmer, laboratory technician, commercial artist, graphic designer, and copyeditor (Grandin, 1999). Environmental issues such as exposure to fluorescent lighting, chemicals, or strong odors are a concern for individuals with sensory sensitivities.

Self-Awareness

Finding a job that is a good fit for the individual's interests and skills requires an examination of personal characteristics and areas of competency. Individuals with social learning disorders should make a list of their positive personal characteristics as well as technical abilities. However, this may be challenging because many of these individuals focus only on their negative qualities.

A strengths-based assessment is important to bring these qualities, such as honesty and loyalty, to their awareness. Most individuals with social learning disorders are honest by nature and would not consider being deceptive; however, they often do not recognize this as a strength.

Individuals with social learning disorders take many of their strong personal characteristics for granted, and these are the very qualities that most employers are looking for in a potential employee. Many of these individuals are perfectionists and persevere until they are satisfied with the quality of their work. Individuals with Asperger syndrome often pay close attention to detail (Happé, 2006), which is an asset in settings that require precision (e.g., editing, laboratory work). In addition, these individuals are more likely to work steadily throughout the day without taking time off to chat or gossip (Howlin, 2004). Gail Hawkins (2004) has suggested that the special interests or fascinations often seen in individuals with ASDs may lead indirectly or directly to a career path. These interests should therefore be recognized and encouraged. There are many exercises one can do to examine personal interests and possible career paths, such as those found in *What Color is Your Parachute?*, a job hunter's guide that is published on a yearly basis (Bolles, 2010). Often interests can be combined to create a satisfying job experience. One young man with Asperger syndrome had a particular expertise with computers and a special interest in automobile makes, models, and statistics. He found employment as a computer technician at a car dealership. Many young women with Asperger syndrome are very drawn to animals. They may choose to pursue veterinary work, animal training, or animal behavior research (Prince-Hughes, 2002).

One's strengths must be considered together with one's areas of difficulty when choosing a job that is a good fit. In his book *Working with Emotional Intelligence*, Daniel Goleman (1998) states that an accurate self-assessment is part of the emotional competence necessary to be successful in the world of work. A person must have an awareness of his or her strengths and limitations (Boyee, 2004).

Although no one is inclined to disclose weaknesses and limitations in a job interview, it is important to think realistically. One young man reported that he took a job at a convenience store where he was expected to cover three areas at once. Although he knew that multitasking was not his strength, he did not admit this in the interview. He only stayed in the job for 1 week because it became too stressful. Some individuals with social learning disorders are not comfortable with teamwork and prefer more individualized tasks. They thrive in environments that are structured and where they are given prescribed tasks daily. In addition, individuals with social learning disorders do not generally seek positions of authority that require them to supervise others. Some may have difficulty receiving or giving criticism. They may also be reluctant to ask for help when they need it (Meyer, 2001). Acknowledging these issues up front can help avoid the pitfalls of jobs that will cause these types of stress.

Temple Grandin (1999) has suggested that certain fields tend to fit well with individuals with ASDs. These areas of specialty include computer science, accounting, engineering, library science, commercial art, photography, equipment design, and journalism—fields that require an attention to detail that is a quality of many individuals with social learning disorders. These jobs also allow for an individualized work environment and involve some aspects of creativity and visual thinking.

The applicant should emphasize his or her special skills to the potential employer. It is recommended that the candidate bring a portfolio of work to highlight areas of expertise (e.g., cartooning, journalism, graphic design, photography, computer game design). A personalized web site is another way to showcase talent. Jobs that require high demands on short-term memory are not recommended, such as being a cashier, waiter, or receptionist in a busy office (Grandin, 1999; Grandin & Duffy, 2004; Hawkins, 2004).

Many young people entering the job market are not aware of how their skills may translate to certain jobs. For example, one individual with a social learning disorder was very gifted at learning foreign languages. He thought his only options were teaching or interpreting. However, many institutions need employees who are bilingual or multilingual. Artistic ability or photography experience is also desirable to many companies and nonprofit organizations. Similarly, knowledge of history or of music may translate into a job at a museum or even doing archival research. These types of skills should always be included in a résumé and even mentioned in initial contact, such as introductory letters or telephone calls.

Interviewing Skills

The interview is often a stumbling block for individuals with social learning disorders. For example, impressions are formed about the candidate based on his social and communication skills, and the interview is a forum for judging how the candidate will interact with other employees. Many people with ASDs cannot get past the interview experience to be hired. They have good qualifications and are often very motivated, but they create a negative impression because of their lack of social skills. As a result, many are underemployed for their level of education and qualifications (Attwood, 2007).

Interviewing skills should be practiced by individuals using a one-way mirror. Participants should be asked to bring in résumés and review them with their coaches, who can act as interviewers. The class should give feedback regarding body language, voice tone, inflection, and eye contact. The participants can also watch themselves on videotape and thereby evaluate their own performance.

Job interview suggestions that have been developed for participants can be found on the accompanying CD-ROM (see Class 11). These suggestions were developed from several resources that provide strategies for successful interviewing and address areas of potential difficulty for individuals with social learning disorders (Adams, 2001; Meyer, 2001). An example would be waiting to call the employer until a week after the interview. Many individuals with social learning disorders are very anxious and may call repeatedly if they are not given any information immediately. Other suggestions involve preparation and organization. The candidate should become knowledgeable about the company or employing organization prior to the interview and then will be able to communicate how his or her experience will match the company's needs. Therefore, participants should be encouraged to maintain a positive attitude throughout the job search process. The job market is very competitive, so participants should expect the job search process to require many attempts before finding employment.

Creating a Positive First Impression

The job interview gives the employer an opportunity to evaluate the candidate based on his or her ability to communicate. The interviewer often asks broad questions that must be answered concisely without long-winded answers. Questions such as "Tell me about yourself" or "Where do you see yourself 5 years from now?" are potentially hazardous if not answered briefly and succinctly. When a candidate is anxious, he or she may tend to either ramble or give very abbreviated answers. The web site http://www.career-journal.com cautions candidates against telling "their life story."

These types of difficult questions should be included in mock interviews. The participants can be given feedback on how to answer questions optimally by answering in a way that highlights their strengths and qualifications. In the book *Developing Talents* (Grandin & Duffy, 2004), the authors suggest practicing a "30-second commercial," in which crucial information about oneself is condensed into 30 seconds. The candidate practices this talk, focusing on the strengths, skills, and goals that are important for the employer to know about him or her. The exercise helps candidates communicate more effectively and increases their self-confidence during the interview. The *Everything Job Interview Book* (Adams, 2001) includes strategies for answering a variety of typical first-interview questions. Participants should be encouraged to practice answering these questions repeatedly until they develop a sense of comfort with the process. This will decrease the likelihood that they will blank on a question or give an inappropriate answer.

Creating a positive impression involves a delicate balance of enthusiasm and self-confidence on the one hand and an appropriate self-view (appropriate modesty) on the other hand. It is important to express interest and enthusiasm about the individual position and the work being done at the company. It is also useful to highlight the skills and experience that make one's background a good fit for the job. However, it is important not to be perceived as overly eager or arrogant.

These fine distinctions are difficult for individuals with social learning disorders and require a great deal of coaching and feedback to be understood. Answering questions with cocky remarks such as "I'm the best engineer you'll ever meet" is a sure way to fail. Thus, although acknowledging one's strengths is important, it must be tempered with humility. Many participants may not have an accurate sense of their skill level and may exaggerate or underrate themselves. An honest presentation of skills should be encouraged, emphasizing areas of training and expressing motivation to continue learning.

Appearing rigid and inflexible can also create negative outcomes in a job interview. Participants should be encouraged to be flexible regarding work hours, but not to agree to conditions that are unacceptable (e.g., varying shifts, both day and night). Most participants will prefer predictable hours and a great deal of structure in the workplace (e.g., set lunch hour and breaks). They will work best in situations where they can develop a routine.

Usually, salary issues are not discussed in an initial interview; however, if the topic is raised by the employer, it is important that the candidate have some idea of what salary range would be appropriate for the job. Salary is often determined by geographic location, years of experience, and various other factors. Some of this information is available in the *Occupational Outlook Handbook* (http://www.bls.gov/oco), which gives the economic outlook for specific professions. It is also advisable to discuss salary range with people outside the company who are currently employed with the same or a very similar job title. Without this type of information, it is difficult to evaluate a salary offer.

Disclosure of Disability

People with social learning disorders do not have to discuss their disability in an initial interview. Hence, it is considered a personal detail about which the employer is prohibited from asking, as are other personal details such as age, religion, nationality, and marital status. It cannot be used as a basis for discrimination.

Although many individuals with social learning disorders do not disclose this information, some have used disclosure with positive results. For example, Lars Perner decided to disclose that he had Asperger syndrome when he was seeking an academic position in marketing analysis. He realized that his poor interviewing skills were often used as a basis to judge his overall abilities. When he indicated that he had Asperger syndrome prior to the interview, he was judged more on his qualifications. He got offers from universities where he had not been successful previously (Diament, 2005).

Although it is not a requirement to reveal that an individual has a diagnosis such as Asperger syndrome, it may be beneficial to provide the employer with information about working style that will facilitate a positive working relationship. When an employee decides to self-disclose a disability, this information must be kept confidential by law (Grandin & Duffy, 2004). Many employers are unfamiliar with social learning disabilities and the challenges they pose in the workplace. It is a proactive strategy to educate employers about the work styles, strengths, and limitations of individuals with social learning disorders.

In his book *Beyond the Wall*, Stephen Shore (2001) created a letter to give to employers that explains the characteristics of an employee with Asperger syndrome. Disclosing a disability is a very personal decision and must be made individually. Many individuals with social learning disorders feel that they are able to be more productive when their employer understands their disability. They can play to their strengths and avoid areas of weakness. Because employees with social learning disorders frequently do not seek feedback and are not likely to ask for clarification, employers need to understand that they must be direct and specific in their communication with them. They cannot assume that they know the "things everyone else knows" (Hawkins, 2004). For some individuals with sensory sensitivities, it is important to receive accommodations, such as a quiet space in which to work. These individuals are often highly annoyed and distracted by open office environments that have little or no defined personal space. They also need solitary time to help them remain focused and reduce the stress of continual interaction with co-workers. Other job environments that require exposure to smells or lighting can be distracting. These factors must all be considered when making the decision to disclose a social learning disability.

Asking for Accommodations

It is important to approach the issue of accommodations with an employer respectfully. Accommodations must be negotiated after the job offer is made. It is important not to present a demanding attitude or appear "entitled." The employer will usually come to an agreement regarding modification of the job description (Meyer, 2001). Although it is important for the employee to advocate for himself or herself, it must be done in a collaborative manner. The employee must work with his or her employer to find the best solution to address workplace concerns. Studies in the United Kingdom (Howlin, 2004) have demonstrated that individuals with ASDs greatly benefit from work environments in which special help is available. Many of the companies employing individuals with high-functioning autism found that providing job coaching was very helpful; indeed, some companies began using these techniques with all new employees (Howlin, 2004). Another option that exists for adults on the autism spectrum is working in enclaves, or a supervised work situation where a group of workers completes a specific amount of work under the supervision of a job coach. The employer makes a fee for task contract and the workers divide the fee under the supervision of an agency that develops the jobs and contracts with the employers (Perry, 2008).

Office Politics

Adults with social learning disorders are often baffled by the complex social interactions among their co-workers, known as office politics. These conflicts, unwritten rules, and power plays are subtle and confusing. Adults with social learning disorders expect directness, but that is not the norm in most work environments. Thus, they are forced to try to ascertain what is implied by their co-workers' behavior.

It is recommended that individuals with social learning disorders seek advice from a trusted friend (not a supervisor) to better understand and navigate office politics. Several autobiographies of adults with ASDs bear out this advice. Both Liane Willey (2001) and Stephen Shore (2001) stress the importance of having a person to give them feedback about their behavior and what would be an appropriate response to certain work-related interpersonal situations. This type of consultation is important to avoid becoming overwhelmed by the intricacies of co-workers' behavior.

Dr. Peter Gerhardt (2000) has suggested that employers consider providing social support and social coaching for employees with social learning disorders. It is important to promote a socially inclusive work environment that may include training co-workers to understand the social and communicative issues of the individual with a social learning disorder.

Class 10: Career Selection and Job Search

The objectives of Class 10 are to

■■ Understand good fit of interests and skills with career goals

■■ Identify skills and interests

■■ Learn effective approaches for a job search

Understand Good Fit of Interests and Skills with Career Goals

Dr. Temple Grandin and other individuals with ASDs have emphasized the importance of finding employment that is a good fit for an individual's strengths and interests. Many of the participants will have very intense interests that can translate into careers. For example, one participant loved commuter trains and buses and had memorized all the schedules for every line. This individual could easily pursue a career in some aspect of transportation management. Another participant loved maps and was able to meet with a cartography company through a parent connection. As noted, a keen interest in animals could lead to a career in veterinary medicine, animal training, or animal behavior research.

It is best for individuals to pursue their true interests rather than what is perceived to be in demand. Many participants are steered into careers that do not fit their personality or are taxing to their social skills, such as sales or teaching. These types of jobs require constant social inter-action and have little downtime. Many individuals need an environment that is relatively quiet where they can work without interruption and some solitary time built into the workday. Another issue is that many jobs require the ability for multitasking, but this is often not an area of strength for individuals with social learning disorders. Some jobs require high demands of short-term memory (e.g., cashier, waiter, receptionist), which can become very stressful. If individuals take one of these jobs because they are feeling pressured, the result is usually negative (termination or they quit on their own).

Many individuals with ASDs fit well in fields that require attention to detail. Some examples of these types of vocations would be computer science, accounting, library science, research, and editing. When researching careers, the book *What Color is Your Parachute?* (Bolles, 2010) can be a great resource for this kind of personal exploration. It is revised every year to keep current with employment trends. The companion workbook also has many exercises for exploring pos-sible careers based on past experience, skills, and interests. There are exercises similar to those developed by Holland (1996), which generate a personality code (e.g., investigative-artistic-so-cial) and the possible career choices that match with the personality type. For example, an inves-tigative personality is analytical, independent, scholarly, and reserved; the possible career choices might be biologist, chemist, historian, physician, or mathematician. Information on Holland code assessments and other career models is available at http://www.hollandcodes.com.

Identify Skills and Interests

Participants may not recognize or may underestimate the importance of their skills (e.g., the abil-ity to speak a foreign language). They may take for granted skills such as being adept with com-puters, artistic ability, or particular knowledge of music or history and not realize these are desir-able in many employment settings. These types of skills should always be included on a résumé or introductory letter. In Handout 11, participants can list technical skills and personal character-istics. This should be done in class so that the participants can share this information with each other. It is important for participants to support each other and point out positive characteristics that have been noticed during class (e.g., punctuality, attention to detail, good verbal skills). Participants should know that it is possible to find jobs that capitalize on their interests and strengths and that it is okay to have a very targeted job search. Handout 12 should be done with social coaches in the last hour of class. Participants should generate a list of their special interests and discuss possible career paths that would correspond.

Resources

There are many resources for learning about different types of employment. The book *What Color Is Your Parachute?* (Bolles, 2010) gives an overview of how to analyze skills and match them to career choices. It also provides statistics on the most successful strategies for finding a job. The vast majority of candidates who successfully find employment made direct contact with the employer by a phone call or visit prior to interviewing. Less than 9% of candidates find a job by submitting a résumé online to a web site such as http://www.monster.com. Personal contact is consistently a factor in success rate (Bolles, 2010).

The *Everything Job Interview Book* (Adams, 2001) provides information on writing cover letters, preparing a résumé, and sending follow-up correspondence. It also has sample job interview questions in various fields, which are helpful in preparing for interviews. Information about companies and possible job openings can be found on http://www.companiesonline.com and http://www.jobfind.com. Many government agencies, organizations, and educational institutions also have web sites that list current job opportunities.

The U.S. Department of Labor Bureau of Labor Statistics (2010) maintains an online listing of job titles. This is a good starting point for individuals who are trying to understand different types of jobs in certain professions such as engineering (e.g., electrical engineering, mechanical engineering, electronic engineering). New job titles are continually created each year as a result of new technologies. Web resources have narrowed down this extensive list to create a more streamlined version. This information may be found at http://www.princetonreview.com/Careers.aspx.

The Internet is a wonderful source of information on jobs and career development. Sites that offer practical advice on job interviewing are http://www.career-journal.com and http://www.job interview.net. Both of these sites list possible interview questions and strategies for answering them optimally. The *Everything Job Interview Book* (Adams, 2001) also lists possible questions for specific fields such as engineering, marketing, or computer programming. These resources may be suggested as supplemental reading to participants. The job search process should be individualized. Therefore, the social coaches should discuss career goals with individual participants at the beginning of this class.

Learn Effective Job Search Strategies

Looking for a job requires lots of effort. It is not enough to send a résumé to an online service such as http://www.monster.com because there are thousands of people doing the same thing. Many individuals with social learning disorders prefer more indirect methods, such as applying online, and do not want to do the networking activities that are often necessary to secure employment in a competitive marketplace. Most of the literature on effective methods for finding a job indicates that the individual must make personal contact with potential employers through letters, e-mails, or telephone calls or by personally dropping off résumés. Networking and getting a name of a contact person inside the company also helps. If there is a friend, neighbor, or family member who knows someone in the company, it is very helpful to use this kind of personal connection.

The majority of individuals who are successful finding a job try to distinguish themselves from other applicants by this kind of contact. One participant found employment by going to a neighborhood barbecue. He had been looking for a job for over a year after graduation but had no success by sending out his résumé and answering internet job postings. His parents insisted that he attend the neighborhood party even though he was reluctant. He met someone there and was discussing his computer skills and interests with this individual. This individual was looking for someone with the participant's skills for a job at his company and hired him on the spot. However, most participants will not be comfortable with a more assertive approach and need some support to initiate this kind of strategy. It is helpful if the social coaches discuss ways that will help get this process started. Generating a list of possible contacts to call or write helps to create daily goals. A daily schedule of job search activities should include follow-up activities, such as calling potential employers back periodically.

Class 11: Job Interviewing

The objectives of Class 11 are to

- Learn effective interviewing skills
- Understand legal and illegal interview questions
- Explore reasons for disclosure
- Practice interview skills

Learn Effective Interviewing Skills

Class 11 emphasizes the importance of being prepared for a job interview. It is critical to know as much as possible about the company before going into the interview, which demonstrates that the candidate is well informed and has self-initiative. If candidates know something about the employer prior to the interview, they can ask informed questions to showcase their knowledge and obtain valuable job information that they might not get otherwise. Of course, employers are also flattered when candidates come prepared, as this indicates to an employer that the job is important to the candidate.

Participants should understand that it is important to answer the interviewer's questions succinctly and not go off on a long-winded response. Dr. Temple Grandin has suggested that individuals create and memorize a 30-second speech that highlights all the important things they want potential employers to know about their job qualifications (Grandin & Duffy, 2004). Other sources such as http://www.career-journal.com suggest creating a similar script that is tailored to a specific employer's interests, goals, and needs. Many people are nervous before and during an interview, so creating a script will help to make sure nothing important gets left out. The script will also reduce some anxiety because there will not be a need to talk spontaneously.

Body language should reflect confidence (e.g., shoulders back, head high, erect posture, direct eye contact) and should be relaxed but formal. Participants should understand that a job interview is not a casual social conversation. It is a structured situation in which it is always better to be formal and polite despite the demeanor of the interviewer. It is not acceptable to use slang terms in an interview, even if the interviewer does. The interviewee should be dressed conservatively regardless of how the interviewer is dressed. Casual dress often sends a negative message to the interviewer that the candidate is too relaxed, so it is always better to err on the side of conservative dress when going to an interview. If the candidate gets the job, then his or her style of dress can be changed according to the prevailing style in the office.

It is also imperative for the participants to arrive 10–15 minutes early for interviews, which provides time for them to settle in and collect themselves before the interview begins. A trial run can be made to the interview location in the days preceding the interview to be sure of directions and traffic volume. If an interviewee is late to a first interview, it sends up a red flag to the interviewer and suggests poor time management skills.

The job applicant should bring extra copies of his or her résumé to the interview. It is also recommended that job candidates think of a few questions to ask during the interview (e.g., "What would a typical workday be like?"). By asking questions, the interviewer gets the impression that the candidate is serious and has really given the position some thought. Finally, the issue of salary should not be brought up by the candidate. Sometimes the employer provides this information in the initial interview, but it should not be discussed until a job offer is made. Some resources for job interviewing can be found online at http://www.career-journal.com and http://www.jobinterview.net. These sites provide sample interview questions and suggested responses. Handout 13 summarizes some job interview suggestions.

Understand Legal and Illegal Questions

Class 11 stresses self-advocacy. It is important to know what types of questions are allowed in an interview so that the participant is not trapped into answering questions that are discriminatory. Participants may not be aware that certain questions are considered illegal and may answer even more personal questions, such as sexual orientation, if asked. It is legal to ask for personal information like a social security number or whether a person has been convicted of a criminal offense (after the age of 18 years). It is also legal for a potential employer to inquire about whether a candidate was terminated from a previous job. The following types of questions are not legal and the candidate does not have to answer them: questions about an individual's marital status, sexual preference, ethnic background, children, or religion. The employer can ask for the individual's age only if the job has a minimum age requirement (e.g., in some states, a person has to be 21 years old to serve alcohol). An employer can only ask about an individual's height or weight if it is pertinent to the performance of a certain job task (e.g., lifting heavy objects). A person with a disability does not have to disclose it in an interview.

Explore Reasons for Disclosure

Many participants with a disability, such as Asperger syndrome or a nonverbal learning disorder, may be concerned about whether disclosing their disability will affect them negatively in a job situation. As previously stated, a disability does not have to be disclosed in an interview, and it is often not to the individual's advantage to disclose this prior to being hired. After an individual is hired, he or she may choose to disclose this information (to the employer or primary supervisor) for the purpose of obtaining some accommodations in the workplace (e.g., a quiet work area free of distractions). Some people feel that disclosing a disability may help create a more beneficial working relationship with the employer and also with co-workers. Others are concerned that this information might be shared with other employees even though it is confidential and only to be known by the employer or direct supervisor according to the Americans with Disabilities Act (ADA) of 1990 (PL 101-336). Disclosure is a personal choice, however, and not all individuals with disabilities will choose to disclose.

Practice Job Interviewing Skills

The last 2 hours of class may be spent practicing job interviewing skills in mock interviews with coaches behind a one-way mirror with the class observing (see Exercise 5). It is suggested that participants bring copies of their résumés to class so that the interviewers have something to work from. Interviews are also videotaped so that the participants can review them. Participants often comment that they learn a lot about their own body language, voice volume, and communication skills through this process. This process will prepare and relax participants for upcoming job interviews. After this initial exercise, the participants should practice again using questions that are more specific to the type of job they are interested in pursuing. It is helpful if they provide this information prior to the class so the coaches can prepare these questions. Sample questions that are typical for specific professions can be found on http://www.jobinterview.net, http://www.careerbuilder.com, http://www.dice.com, http://www.computerwork.com, and various other web resources.

Exercise 5. Social Coaching Exercise

Participants should discuss the types of jobs they are interested in and then practice the following job interview questions with their coaches. When responding, participants should try to answer questions concisely without being lengthy, focus on selling themselves by emphasizing what they have to offer the company, discuss their accomplishments and areas of strength, use examples to illustrate their skills, be aware of their body language (e.g., smile, lean forward, make eye contact, be an "active" listener by nodding, show interest through facial expressions), and not disclose too much personal information (e.g., not talk at length about family).

How has your education/experience prepared you for this position?

What are your strengths?

What are your weaknesses?

What kinds of extracurricular activities (hobbies) are you involved in?

Where do you see yourself in 5 years?

Why should I hire you?

Handout 11: Listing Personal Characteristics and Technical Abilities

In one column, list personal characteristics that make you a good candidate for employment. Integrity, loyalty, and creativity are examples of personal characteristics. In the other column, list your technical skills. Examples would be typing speed, photography or the ability to develop film, knowledge of computer programs, or the ability to speak a foreign language.

Personal characteristics	Technical skills

Handout 12: Interest List and Related Jobs

Make a list of your special interests. If you are interested in a particular topic such as movies, please list all aspects of movies that interest you (e.g., special effects, editing, set design). With your social coach, generate a list of jobs that are related to your interest. For example, if your interest is movies, you may list jobs such as working in a movie theater, working for a film festival (e.g., Philadelphia Film Festival, Tribeca Film Festival), or being a movie critic.

Source: Hawkins (2004).

- Learn all you can about the company or organization.

- Be prepared to answer and ask questions.

- Prepare your clothes; select business attire (e.g., suit, coat and tie).

- Bring extra copies of your résumé and reference letters.

- Arrive 10–15 minutes early.

- Maintain a professional image; for example, do not act casual, use slang, or address the interviewer by his or her first name.

- Do not interrupt the interviewer.

- Be aware of your nonverbal behaviors and pay attention to the interviewer's body language.

- Be enthusiastic, confident, and energetic.

- Listen carefully.

- At the end of the interview, make sure you understand the employer's next step.

- Send a thank you letter to the employer, emphasizing what you have to offer.

- Do not call the employer immediately (e.g., if the interviewer says the company will be making a decision in a week, it is acceptable to call after a week).

8

■■■■■

▋ The College Experience

■■■■■ Lars Perner, a professor of marketing who has Asperger syndrome, has said that college is a place where "being nerdy is cool" (2002, p. 1). The college environment is a place where intellect is valued and offers the opportunity for meeting like-minded people and forming community. Although college can be an ideal place for those who are academically inclined, there are many social demands. For example, the difficulty of living away from home, increased responsibilities, and less structure are a part of college life. Many individuals with social learning disorders find the social world of college overwhelming. Dormitory life can be frustrating for those who need solitary time. Also, college success requires the ability to be organized. These issues are all important considerations when choosing a college. Temple Grandin (1999) has recommended that high school students take classes focused on special interests (e.g., computers, languages) at community colleges during high school and in the summer before starting college, which helps to make the transition to college smoother.

Students who have received special education services throughout elementary, middle, and high school are often unaware that their individualized education program (IEP) does not continue in the college setting. Instead, colleges and universities often require an independent evaluation of the disability, which is usually done by a psychologist (and usually not paid for by the school district). The Individuals with Disabilities Education Improvement Act (IDEA) of 2004 (PL 108-446) requires that students receive a summary of performance from their school that outlines the students' strengths, weaknesses, and need for accommodations. This document serves as a proof of a student's need for accommodations; however, a college or university may still require an independent evaluation.

Many colleges now provide learning support to students; however, the services offered vary widely. In addition, colleges often provide certain accommodations for students who can provide documentation of a disability (e.g., taking a reduced course load, having untimed tests, taking tests separately to reduce distractions). Supports such as these and any other accommodations for people with disabilities are monitored and offered under the Americans with Disabilities Act (ADA) of 1990 (PL 101-336). Students can find out more about how to access these accommodations at college by visiting the Office of Disability Supports or Services on campus.

Individuals with social learning disorders may also require accommodations in areas such as dormitory life. Students may request a single room or have a specially selected roommate. A list of colleges and universities that have experience with students with social learning disorders and provide these types of accommodations is available online at the Asperger Foundation International web site (http://www.aspfi.org). The Penn Autism Network web site (http://www.med.upenn.edu/pan) is just one of many web sites that provides extensive information on college resources for students with disabilities. The web site contains many articles that address the experiences of students with social learning disorders and how colleges are providing special accommodations (e.g., Marshall University's Asperger program). The Global and Regional Asperger Syndrome Partnership and the Organization for Autism Research (n.d.) have created a video that explains the challenges that students with Asperger syndrome may have in the classroom and provides some suggestions for accommodations. Coulter (2003, 2005) offers other resources for students entering college.

Although it is important not to overwhelm those students who are socially uncomfortable, it is equally important not to foster social disconnection and isolation. Sitting in a dormitory room playing video games alone does not enhance social competency. Students with social learning disorders should be encouraged to join campus organizations that are of interest, which will provide an opportunity to meet others in a structured setting. Many participants may find this to be a less stressful way to become socially involved in campus life. Dr. Scott Robertson, an individual with Asperger syndrome, found that he spent most of his time sitting alone in his dormitory room until he got involved reporting for the university paper. He said this opened up a whole social world that he would never have experienced otherwise (Robertson, 2008).

Students with social learning disorders may function better in a smaller college, which may be less socially overwhelming. However, some students prefer the anonymity of a large campus and tend to socialize with a small number of students in their area of study. Other students may choose to live off campus. Universities may provide a contact person, usually a staff member or postgraduate student, to provide support and advice to students with social learning disorders. Universities may also have support networks for isolated students, which can provide tutorial and study groups as well as recreational activities. Student mentors often can assist these students with managing finances and everyday living skills such as shopping and doing laundry (Berney, 2004).

Several colleges and universities have developed specific programs to address these college adjustment issues. Drexel University, Marshall University, and the University of Arizona provide comprehensive programs for new students with Asperger syndrome. The University of Arizona program specifically focuses on providing social skills training. The University of Alabama has developed a college transition program for students with Asperger syndrome, which provides individual and group sessions for freshmen. Fairleigh Dickinson University has a program to assist students with organizational skills, independent living, and the challenges of social life in college.

Another option available to students with social learning disorders is specialized independent living programs. Programs such as the College Internship Program (various locations; see http://www.collegeinternshipprogram.com) and the College Living Experience (various locations; see http://www.cleinc.net) provide social mentoring, a specific curriculum, and more structure while still allowing independence. Other similar programs include The Allen Institute Center for Innovative Learning in Connecticut, The Horizons School in Alabama, The New York Institute of Technology Vocational Independence Program, and the Threshold Program in Massachusetts.

Class 12: Final Class Party

The objectives of Class 12 are to

- Use skills learned in a party setting
- Converse with strangers
- Establish connections for after class

Class 12 was added at the request of previous class participants who wanted to improve their skills interacting with a group of people in a party atmosphere. This situation was something that they had avoided in the past, but they wanted to know how to feel more comfortable socializing with a number of people that they did not know—a typical situation at college parties. Coaches should invite additional guests to the class so that the participants have the opportunity to initiate conversations with people they do not already know. The party should be casual and can be held in the university's student center or similar setting. No alcohol should be served, but there can be plenty of food and the atmosphere should be festive.

This should be a celebration of class accomplishments, so the mood will be generally positive for most participants. They have practiced conversation skills with their coaches and should feel better prepared to initiate or respond to overtures to converse. That being said, there will invariably be some students who are anxious about socializing and will need some prompting and support from the social coaches. This should also be an opportunity for the participants to establish connections with each other by exchanging e-mail addresses and telephone numbers. Previous class participants may also be invited to reconnect with instructors, coaches, and other participants.

As an alternative to the class party, the final class can meet at a family-style restaurant where dishes are shared. It may be best to request a separate area of the restaurant that is less noisy so the class members are not distracted by this. This setting will increase interaction among the class members. Each coach should bring a friend so there are new people with whom the participants can meet and interact.

9

Demographics and Outcome Measures

Since 2003, the Penn Social Skills Program has taught the Social Skills Seminar on a continuous basis and had more than 300 participants from the Philadelphia metropolitan area, including parts of New Jersey and Delaware. The course has also been offered in New York City and suburban Philadelphia since 2009. The program's participants have included 179 men (84%) and 27 women (16%), with a median age of 24 years. Some participants were older than 35 years. Diagnoses included Asperger syndrome (78%), social phobia (9%), nonverbal learning disability (8%), and other co-morbid diagnoses, such as attention-deficit/hyperactivity disorder and obsessive-compulsive disorder (5%). All participants were of average to above-average and superior intelligence. About 19% of the participants were employed and 54% were either full-time or part-time students. About 27% had graduate or professional school degrees.

Outcome Measures

Since the creation of the program, research on outcome measures has been a goal. The evaluation of the program is ongoing to determine the most effective elements of the curriculum. For example, social coaches are evaluated by the participants, and the coaches provide an evaluation of their experience in the program. Preprogram and postprogram measures were obtained from the participants and their parents. The participants completed the Friendship Questionnaire (Baron-Cohen & Wheelwright, 2003) and the Empathy Quotient (Baron-Cohen & Wheelwright, 2004) before and after the program. Parents were asked to complete the Social Responsiveness Scale–Adult Version (Constantino et al., 2003) before and after the program.

The following two studies were done in 2006 and 2009, respectively, to look at the program's effectiveness in increasing motivation to socialize, increasing empathy in the first and decreasing social anxiety in the second. These studies were presented at the American Psychological Association Convention in San Francisco, California, and the Second and Third Social Brain Conferences in Glasgow, Scotland.

Efficacy of Social Skills Training for Adults with Asperger Syndrome

Some research has been conducted with participants in social skills training courses. The effectiveness of this social skills seminar has been examined in two areas: motivation to seek out relationships and the ability to understand other people's feelings and intentions. Cohen, Rostain, Brodkin, and Sankoorikal (2006) wanted to assess the effectiveness of a 10-week social skills training curriculum for adults with Asperger syndrome that focused on communication, job interview, and interpersonal skills. Adults with Asperger syndrome have unique social difficulties that interfere with their ability to communicate effectively, find employment, and develop meaningful interpersonal relationships. Similar to the program featured in this book, the curriculum in this study utilized an experiential training model, which provided practice of skills outside the classroom with individual social coaches. The course consisted of 15 hours of classroom instruction and 10 hours of individual practice with coaches.

In this study, 39 participants diagnosed with Asperger syndrome completed a self-assessment of their social skills using the Empathy Quotient (Baron-Cohen & Wheelwright, 2004) and Friendship Questionnaire (Baron-Cohen & Wheelwright, 2003) at the beginning and end of the course. Parents of the participants completed the Social Responsiveness Scale–Adult Version (Constantino et al., 2003) prior to the course and at the conclusion, which provided another measure of sociability from the perspective of a family member.

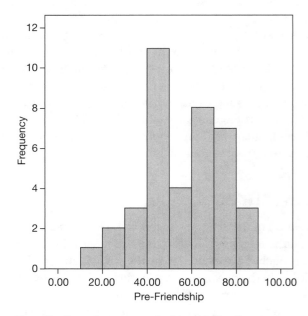

Figure 2. Preprogram scores on the Friendship Questionnaire (Baron-Cohen & Wheelwright, 2003) (mean = 55.8205, standard deviation = 16.90978, number = 39). (*Source:* Cohen, Rostain, Brodkin, & Sankoorikal, 2006.)

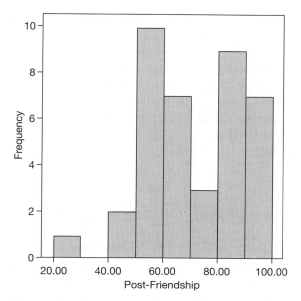

Figure 3. Postprogram scores on the Friendship Questionnaire (Baron-Cohen & Wheelwright, 2003) (mean = 70.3333, standard deviation = 17.35441, number = 39). (*Source:* Cohen, Rostain, Brodkin, & Sankoorikal, 2006.)

A paired *t*-test analysis of both preprogram and postprogram scores on the Empathy Quotient revealed a 4-point increase in empathy from 27 to 31, which indicates that participants demonstrated an increased ability to understand other people's feelings and intentions after completing the program. A paired *t*-test analysis of preprogram and postprogram scores on the Friendship Questionnaire indicated that scores increased from 56 to 70, suggesting increased interaction with others and interest in people after completing the program (see Figures 2 and 3). Finally, results of the *t*-test analysis for preprogram and postprogram scores on the Social Responsiveness Scale found lower scores after completion of the course, indicating increased social awareness, reciprocal social responses, and reduced social anxiety (see Figure 4). Therefore, it can be concluded that a curriculum specifically designed to address social difficulties of adults with social learning disorders can produce an increased interest in people, improvement in interpersonal relationships, and increased motivation to socialize.

The results of the Friendship Questionnaire suggest that participants' attitudes toward friendship and the motivation to seek out new relationships increased during the program. The curriculum emphasized self-esteem through successful social experiences and the supportive relationship with a peer social coach. Skill acquisition in areas such as conversation may have produced a sense of social competence that was lacking before the program. The participants likely

		Paired Differences							
		Mean	Standard Deviation	Standard Error Mean	95% Confidence Interval of the Difference		*t*	*df*	Sig. (2-tailed)
					Lower	Upper			
Pair 1	Pre-Post	−14.51282	13.46706	2.15646	−18.87834	−10.14731	−6.730	38	.000

Figure 4. Paired samples test. (*Source:* Cohen, Rostain, Brodkin, & Sankoorikal, 2006.) (*Key:* Sig., significance.)

Table 1. Study comparison of Empathy Quotient mean scores (Baron-Cohen & Wheelwright, 2004)

Study	Empathy Quotient (mean score)
Baron-Cohen and Wheelwright (2004)	
Participants with social learning disorders	20.4
Control subjects	42.1
Cohen, Rostain, Brodkin, and Sankoorikal (2006)	
Participants before completing the program	26.6
Participants after completing the program	30.9

had more motivation to socialize and therefore took social risks because their self-image was improved.

The construct of empathy, as defined as the ability to understand another person's feelings and motivations and form an appropriate affective response, seemed to be less influenced by participation in the training course. A core difficulty of social perception and cognition requires a long-term approach. The participants in this social skills training program came in with higher mean scores on the Empathy Quotient than participants in another study (Baron-Cohen & Wheelwright, 2004). The results suggest that incremental gains are slow and may require intensive instruction over a long period. A comparison of these studies is presented in Table 1.

Efficacy of a Social Skills Training Intervention to Reduce Social Anxiety and Increase Social Motivation

Young adults with ASDs have unique social difficulties that interfere with their abilities to communicate effectively, find employment, and develop meaningful interpersonal relationships. Many of these individuals cannot process nonverbal social cues (e.g., facial expressions, body language) and report high levels of social anxiety. Although various social skills training programs have been developed for children and young adolescents with ASDs, this has not been the case for young adults. One study examined the feasibility and effectiveness of a 12-week social skills training program employing both group sessions and individualized social coaching for reducing social anxiety and increasing social motivation in young adults with ASDs (Cohen, Rostain, & Dahlsgaard, 2010). Program participants were administered the Social Interaction Anxiety Scale (SIAS; Mattick & Clarke, 1998) and the Friendship Questionnaire (Baron-Cohen & Wheelwright, 2003) before and after completion of the social skills training program. Results indicated the presence of considerable social anxiety among the participants and suggested a significant effect of the training intervention in reducing reported levels of social interaction anxiety and increasing motivation to socialize.

All individuals participated in the social skills seminar for 3 hours weekly for a period of 12 weeks (36 total hours). Each participant worked individually with an assigned social coach on a weekly basis. Participants completed the SIAS prior to and at the completion of the program. This self-report scale consists of 20 items that measure an individual's fears of general social interaction. Individuals indicate on a Likert scale of 0–4 whether an item is not at all characteristic to extremely characteristic of them. Total scores may range from 0 to 80. In the validation study, the clinical group (social phobia) had a mean score of 34.6 and the community sample mean score was 18.8. In addition, participants completed the Friendship Questionnaire, a 35-item self-report

Table 2. Mean scores, standard deviations, and correlations for the Friendship Questionnaire (Baron-Cohen & Wheelwright, 2003) and Social Interaction Anxiety Scale (SIAS; Mattick & Clarke, 1998) before and after the program

	Friendship Questionnaire		Social Interaction Anxiety Scale	
	Preprogram	Postprogram	Preprogram	Postprogram
Preprogram Friendship Questionnaire (SD)	53.95 mean (15.74) SD	.72* r	−.27 r	−.28 r
Postprogram Friendship Questionnaire (SD)		67.55 mean (16.72) SD	−.32 r	−.23 r
Preprogram Social Interaction Anxiety Scale (SD)			40.63 (13.64)	.92*
Postprogram Social Interaction Anxiety Scale (SD)				32.88 (12.15)

Key: SD, standard deviation; r, correlation; *, statistically significant correlation.

instrument that measures the perceived importance of friendships, interest in people, and motivation to socialize. Total scores may range from 0 to 135. In the original Friendship Questionnaire validation study, the mean scores of men and women with ASDs were 53.2 and 59.8, respectively, as compared with mean scores of 70.3 and 90.0 for the men and women without ASDs who were control subjects (Baron-Cohen & Wheelwright, 2003).

The results of the study are presented in Table 2. The preprogram Friendship Questionnaire mean score was 54.0 (range, 16–81), which was quite similar to that reported for individuals with ASDs in the study by Baron-Cohen and Wheelwright (2003). The postprogram Friendship Questionnaire mean score was 67.6 (range, 27–95). Results of repeated measures analyses of variance reveal that Friendship Questionnaire scores increased significantly from before to after the program, with a large effect size ($F(1, 39) = 48.97$, $p < .001$, $\eta^2 = .56$). The preprogram SIAS mean score was 40.6 (range, 14–60) and the postprogram SIAS mean score was 32.9 (range, 11–53). (Recall that for the SIAS, lower scores indicate less social anxiety.) Both scores indicate considerable social interaction anxiety (Mattick & Clarke, 1998). SIAS scores decreased significantly from before to after the program with a large effect size ($F(1, 39) = 84.76$, $p < .001$, $\eta^2 = .69$).

The intercorrelations among all measures are also shown in Table 2, with predictive r values printed in bold. Not surprisingly, the largest r values were those between same measures before and after the program (Friendship Questionnaire = .72; SIAS = .92). Only the aforementioned r values reached significance at $p < .008$, the level set by a Bonferonni correction for the number of r values calculated. As expected, cross-measure r values were negative, although small in magnitude and nonsignificant. The participants appear to have experienced a significant increase in motivation to socialize and decrease in their social anxiety after taking the course. However, there was no relationship found between the level of anxiety reduction and an increase in the level of motivation to socialize in the participants.

This study sought to examine the efficacy of a social skills training intervention to reduce social anxiety and increase social motivation in young adults with ASDs, a growing population with limited research in the area of intervention. Results demonstrate that the social skills seminar intervention can improve motivation to socialize and reduce social anxiety in this population. These results and others show that evidence-based treatments for social learning disorders can be integrated into effectual social skills interventions for ASDs (e.g., Cardaciotto & Herbert, 2004) and confirm the feasibility of such an intervention in a regular clinical setting with adults.

To the best of our knowledge, this was the first social skills intervention study with adults with ASDs to record changes in social anxiety using a standardized, well-validated measure. All participants had a primary diagnosis of Asperger syndrome but also reported levels of social interaction anxiety equivalent to a previous sample of adults diagnosed with social phobia (Mattick & Carke, 1998). Previous literature and clinical accounts of ASDs have raised the question of whether the core social difficulties lead inexorably to social anxiety or are maintained by a concomitant lack of interest in engaging with others, which in turn raises the question of which should be targeted in social skills interventions (Ramsay et al., 2005). After participating in the Social Skills Seminar, participants reported significantly decreased social interaction anxiety on the SIAS and significantly increased motivation to socialize on the Friendship Questionnaire. The correlations between the measures, although negative, were small in magnitude and not significant. This suggests that the measures are tapping related but distinct constructs and indicates that social skills interventions for individuals with ASDs need to target both.

Hypothesized mechanisms of this effect include exposure and desensitization to social situations, immediate feedback, positive reinforcement, and cognitive change. The program used a group format, which provided the participants with an opportunity for social exposure, as well as to form social bonds with other class members and social coaches. Each participant also had individualized instruction with a social coach, practicing specific social behaviors both in the classroom and in natural settings. For many participants, this may have been the first positive peer relationship they experienced. The instructors and social coaches provided immediate self-corrective feedback to the participants based on real-time observations. The participants also received positive reinforcement in class as well as encouragement from their social coaches for attempting to perform tasks (approach behavior).

Participants experienced reduced negative attributional bias as their social skills improved. The cognitive shift that occurred during the course was evidenced by participants' spontaneous comments (e.g., "Before the program, I only noticed unfriendly people; now I notice the people smiling at me"). The class used a cognitive-behavioral approach to alter negative antecedent cognitive reappraisals when confronting social situations, thereby discouraging avoidance behaviors. The participants began to adopt positive cognitions about their abilities to be successful in social settings as their sense of social competency improved (Bandura, 1977).

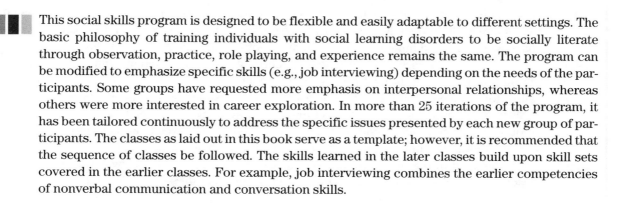

10

Practical Applications

This social skills program is designed to be flexible and easily adaptable to different settings. The basic philosophy of training individuals with social learning disorders to be socially literate through observation, practice, role playing, and experience remains the same. The program can be modified to emphasize specific skills (e.g., job interviewing) depending on the needs of the participants. Some groups have requested more emphasis on interpersonal relationships, whereas others were more interested in career exploration. In more than 25 iterations of the program, it has been tailored continuously to address the specific issues presented by each new group of participants. The classes as laid out in this book serve as a template; however, it is recommended that the sequence of classes be followed. The skills learned in the later classes build upon skill sets covered in the earlier classes. For example, job interviewing combines the earlier competencies of nonverbal communication and conversation skills.

Classroom Modifications

This program was taught for 6 years using a classroom that had a one-way mirror and videotaping capability. When the New York class started, there was no space available with a one-way mirror. Instead, the class used a psychodrama room that contained a small upraised stage and lighting. This arrangement worked very well for role playing. The lighting was useful for concealing the observers from the actors and therefore functioned similar to a one-way mirror. The large space also afforded more opportunity for movement exercises, such as speed conversations. It is also helpful to have space for the improvisational exercises described later in this chapter. The class could be held in a school or office conference room or cafeteria where furniture can be arranged for role-play and observation exercises.

Age Modifications

Although the program was originally designed to address the challenges of transition to adulthood faced by young adults, it has been used successfully for adults in their 30s, 40s, and 50s. The older groups are often more interested in job interviewing skills because of dissatisfaction with their current or past employment. The curriculum therefore can be modified to spend three to four classes on careers and employment issues. When working with older groups, exercises should be relevant to the age group. For example, relatively few older adults use Facebook for social networking. Instead, they may be more interested in learning how to use more traditional dating sites such as http://www.match.com or http://www.eharmony.com. Younger groups may be specifically concentrated on interpersonal skills such as dating and Internet use. These modifications should be agreed upon by the participants early in the course instruction. The instructor may also adjust the course emphasis to nonverbal communication if it is determined to be the greatest area of need for the participants.

Skill Level Modifications

The program was designed for college-educated and college-bound participants. However, participants may have a lower level of education. All written materials require a sixth-grade reading level and are enhanced by the visual presentation on the slides. The visual representations (e.g., body language images) are essential for comprehension for groups with lower skill levels. For these groups, more emphasis should be placed on nonverbal communication and basic conversation skills. This can be expanded by adding additional visual materials such as television and silent movie clips. The television shows *Third Rock from the Sun* and *The Big Bang Theory* often have wonderful and humorous representations of socially inappropriate behaviors.

Adolescent classes may use a modified curriculum (10 weeks) that eliminates Classes 10 and 11 on job search and interviewing skills. The course may also be reduced to 2 hours weekly to allow for reduced attention span. Adolescents often respond best to an emphasis on visual materials that feature teen-oriented themes and actors. The class has been taught to many adolescent groups in private practice and school settings. A modified 6-week class has been piloted at two universities and a community college for incoming freshmen with social concerns.

A version of the program that consists of only the first 6 classes was successfully used to teach social skills to older adults with social learning disorders. For older adults, the class length can be shortened and class exercises repeated several times.

Using Acting Techniques

The use of acting techniques is often suggested to increase the participants' social awareness. Dr. Carol Moog, a psychologist who has been teaching the Social Skills Seminar, has drawn upon her acting background to incorporate improvisation exercises into the class. She has suggested use of these techniques to create movement and body awareness in individuals with social learning disorders who often appear rigid and unexpressive. These individuals may not know how to relax their bodies and need to learn to "go with the flow" of social activity. These exercises serve the dual purpose of increasing body flexibility while creating a nonthreatening, playful atmosphere in the class. Exercise 2 on mirroring (discussed in Chapter 4) is a good way to introduce the concept of body awareness to participants so that they can become more aware of other people's body movements, gestures, and facial expressions as well as their own. This activity can also break down the barriers of the members' self-consciousness and therefore is a good initial class activity. The following are some exercises suggested by Dr. Moog (personal communication, June 12, 2009):

- *Eye contact:* Have two people engage in conversation while looking at the floor. This emphasizes the importance of eye contact in creating a feeling of attunement between the two. A variation on this theme is to have one person attempt to make eye contact while the other looks away.

- *Greetings:* Divide the class into pairs and have the pairs walk toward each other and only make brief eye contact. Then have the pairs repeat the exercise making brief eye contact and saying "hello" to each other. This process can continue, adding more interaction progressively each time. This type of gradual exercise helps the members become more comfortable with increased social interaction without overwhelming them.

- *Facial expression:* Divide the class into pairs. Pair A should have their eyes closed, whereas Pair B should assume a neutral or nonexpressive face. Pair A opens their eyes and has to decide how their Pair B partner is feeling. This emphasizes the importance of facial expression in people's initial reactions when meeting or interacting socially.

- *Humor:* The use of humor also reduces anxiety and can be integrated into conversation exercises by having coaches portray funny characters. This was used extensively in a class for which one of the assistants was also an actor. He took on various humorous personas during conversational role playing. This often resulted in the class members being less reluctant to participate in role playing. They even began volunteering!

Dr. Moog has also used humorous clips from television shows that emphasize negative social behaviors. For instance, after watching a *Saturday Night Live* clip about "Dating the Self-Conscious" (O'Donoghue et al., 1977) in which two highly self-conscious people on a date display a variety of nervous behaviors, this class is asked to give their impressions of the characters.

Dr. Moog has also found it important to "meet students where they are" when it comes to getting them to participate in role playing or other exercises. If a student is self-conscious and does not feel comfortable being in front of the class, she asks the student to do the role play at his or her seat and has the class come to the student.

Finding Social Coaches

Coaches can be recruited through postings on a web site, as well as through a university's departments of social work, education, and psychology and its medical school. Although potential coaches are relatively easy to recruit on college campuses, many settings such as private practices do not have them readily available. It is recommended that community agencies or private practice settings recruit graduate school interns from departments of education, psychology, or social work as coaches who can fulfill internship/externship requirements through their participation in the program. Some high schools also have social work and psychology interns who can serve as social coaches.

Concluding Thoughts

This book encompasses 8 years of experience in teaching individuals with social learning disorders the concept of social literacy. It is the culmination of many years of research combining the existing data on social cognition and social learning with what is currently known about the social impairments of individuals with ASDs, nonverbal learning disorders, and social anxiety. The program has continuously evolved in that time period and will continue to in our ever-changing society. It has developed through the contributions of the many who have participated as students, instructors, and coaches. Becoming socially literate can provide opportunities for new relationships and break the cycle of social avoidance and isolation. Social literacy also enhances existing relationships as communication improves and understanding increases. In addition, those who are socially literate will have more success finding employment and having positive relationships in the workplace. It is hoped that this program will continue to help individuals who have struggled socially in the past to have the skills necessary to achieve their future goals.

References

Adams, B. (2001). *The everything job interview book.* Avon, MA: Adams Media Corporation.

American Psychiatric Association. (2000). *Diagnostic and statistical manual of mental disorders* (4th ed., text rev.) Washington, DC: Author.

Americans with Disabilities Act (ADA) of 1990, PL 101-336, 42 U.S.C. §§ 12101 *et seq.*

Anckarsäter, H., Stahlberg, O., Larson, T., Hakansson, C., Sig-Britt, J., Niklasson, L., et al. (2006). The impact of ADHD and autism spectrum disorders on temperament, character, and personality development. *American Journal of Psychiatry, 163,* 1239–1244.

Antony, M.M., & Swinson, R.P. (2000a). *Phobic disorders and panic in adults: A guide to assessment and treatment.* Washington, DC: American Psychological Association.

Antony, M.M., & Swinson, R.P. (2000b). *The shyness and social anxiety workbook.* Oakland, CA: New Harbinger Publications.

Attwood, T. (2003). Frameworks for behavioral interventions. *Child and Adolescent Psychiatric Clinics of North America, 12,* 65–86.

Attwood, T. (2007). *The complete guide to Asperger's syndrome.* Philadelphia: Jessica Kingsley Publishers.

Attwood, T. (2009). Understanding and teaching friendship skills. Retrieved November 4, 2009, from http://www.tonyattwood.com.au

Avis, J. & Harris, P. (1991). Belief desire reasoning among Baka children: Evidence for a universal conception of mind. *Child Development, 62*(3), 460–467.

Bandura, A. (1977). *Social learning theory.* Englewood Cliffs, NJ: Prentice-Hall.

Baron-Cohen, S. (2004a). *The essential difference.* New York: Basic Books.

Baron-Cohen, S. (2004b). *Mind reading emotions library* [CD-ROM]. Philadelphia: Jessica Kingsley Publishers.

Baron-Cohen, S. (2005). *The hyper-systemizing theory of autism.* AWARES Conference Autism 2005. Retrieved October 14, 2005, from http://awares.org/conferences.

Baron-Cohen, S., & Wheelwright, S. (2003). The Friendship Questionnaire: An investigation of adults with Asperger Syndrome or high-functioning autism, and normal sex differences. *Journal of Autism and Developmental Disorders, 33*(5), 509–517.

Baron-Cohen, S., & Wheelwright, S. (2004). The Empathy Quotient: An investigation of adults with Asperger Syndrome or high-functioning autism, and normal sex differences. *Journal of Autism and Developmental Disorders, 34*(2), 163–175.

Beck, J. (1995). *Cognitive therapy: Basics and beyond.* New York: Guilford Press.

Berney, T. (2004). Asperger Syndrome from childhood into adulthood. *Advances in Psychiatric Treatment, 10,* 341–351.

Blakemore, S., Winston, J., & Frith, U. (2004). Social cognitive neuroscience: Where are we heading? *TRENDS in Cognitive Sciences, 8*(5), 216–222.

Bogdashina, O. (2003). *Sensory perceptual issues in autism and Asperger syndrome: Different sensory experiences, different perceptual worlds.* Philadelphia: Jessica Kingsley Publishers.

Bolles, R.N. (2005). *What color is your parachute? A practical manual for job-hunters and career-changers.* Berkeley, CA: Ten Speed Press.

Bolles, R.N. (2010). *What color is your parachute? A practical manual for job-hunters and career-changers.* Berkeley, CA: Ten Speed Press.

Boyee, J.P. (2004). *Getting and keeping jobs: Employment and people with autism.* Retrieved January 26, 2005, from http://trainland.tripod.com/jeanpaul.htm

Brown, D. (2008, July 11). Mental activity may affect autism-linked genes. *The Washington Post,* p. A02.

Brown, D., Golden, K., & Holleran, L. (Producers), & Hallström, L. (Director). (2000). *Chocolat* [Motion picture]. United States: Miramax.

Cardaciotto, L., & Herbert, J.D. (2004). Cognitive behavior therapy for social anxiety disorder in the context of Asperger's syndrome: A single-subject report. *Cognitive and Behavioral Practice, 11,* 75–81.

Carr, L., Iacoboni, M., Dubeau, M.C., Mazziotta, J.C., & Lenzi, G.L. (2003). Neural mechanisms of empathy in humans: A relay from neural systems for imitation to limbic areas. *Proceedings of the National Academy of Science U S A, 100,* 5497–5502.

Castle Rock Entertainment (Producer), & Reiner, R. (Director). *When Harry met Sally* [Motion picture]. United States: Nelson Entertainment.

Cath, D.C., Ran, N., Smit, H.H., van Balkdom, A., & Comijs, H.C. (2008). Symptom overlap between autism spectrum disorder, generalized social anxiety disorder, and obsessive-compulsive disorder in adults: A preliminary case-controlled study. *Psychopathology, 41,* 101–110.

Cederlund, M., & Gillberg, C. (2004). One hundred males with Asperger syndrome: a clinical study of background and associated factors. *Developmental Medicine and Child Neurology, 46,* 652–661.

Chalfant, A.M., Rapee, R., & Carroll, L. (2007). Treating anxiety disorders in children with high functioning autism spectrum disorders: A controlled trial. *Journal of Autism and Developmental Disorders, 37,* 1842–1857.

Cohen, M.R., Rostain, A.L., Brodkin, E., & Sankoorikal, G. (2006). *Efficacy of social skills training for adult males with Asperger Syndrome*. Poster session presented at the Social Brain 2 International Conference, Glasgow, Scotland.

Cohen, M.R., Rostain, A.L., & Dahlsgaard, K. (2010). *Efficacy of a social skills training intervention to reduce social anxiety and increase social motivation in young adults with autism spectrum disorders*. Poster session presented at Social Brain 3, International Conference, Glasgow, Scotland.

Constantino, J., Davis, S., Todd, R., Schindler, M., Gross, M., Brophy, S., et al. (2003). Validation of a brief quantitative measure of autistic traits: Comparison of the Social Responsiveness Scale with the Autism Diagnostic Interview–Revised. *Journal of Autism and Developmental Disorders, 33*(4), 427–433.

Copeland, S., McCall, J., Williams, C., Guth, C., Carter, E., Presley, J., et al. (2004). High school peer buddies: A win-win situation. *Teaching Exceptional Children, 35*, 16-21.

Costanzo, M., & Archer, D. (1993). *The Interpersonal Perception Task-15* (IPT-15) [Video]. Berkeley, CA: Berkeley Media.

Coulter, J. (2003). *First year at college: Lessons learned*. Retrieved November 18, 2010, from http://www.coulter video.com/FirstyrCollegeessay.htm

Coulter, J. (2005). *Autism spectrum disorders and choosing college courses*. Retrieved November 18, 2010, from http://www.coultervideo.com/collegecourses.htm

Courchesne, E. & Pierce, K. (2005). Why the frontal cortex in autism might be talking only to itself: local over-connectivity but long-distance disconnection. *Current Opinion in Neurobiology, 15*, 225–230.

Darwin, C. (1871). *The descent of man, and selection in relation to sex*. London: John Murray.

Diament, M. (2005, October 14). A secret syndrome. *The Chronicle of Higher Education*, 10–12.

Dingfelder, S. (2005). Autism's smoking gun? *American Psychological Association Monitor, 36*(9), 52–56.

Dunbar, R.I.M. (1992). Neocortex size as a constraint on group size in primates. *Journal of Human Evolution, 20*, 469–493.

Ekman, P. (2003). *Emotions revealed*. New York: Henry Holt and Company.

Ekman, P. (2009). *F.A.C.E. training*. Retrieved July 8, 2010, from http://face.paulekman.com/productdetail.aspx?pid=28

Ekman, P., & Friesen, W.V. (2003). *Unmasking the face*. Cambridge, MA: Malor Books.

Ekroth, L. (2004). *Small talk success tips*. Las Vegas, NV: Working Knowledge Press.

Eryilmaz, D., & Darn, S. (2005). *Non-verbal communication*. Retrieved November 3, 2005, from http://www.teaching english.org.uk/think/methodology/nonverbal.shtml

Fast, Y. (2004). *Employment for individuals with Asperger syndrome or non-verbal learning disability*. Philadelphia: Jessica Kingsley Publishers.

Fitzgerald, M. (2005). *The genesis of artistic creativity: Asperger's syndrome and the arts*. Philadelphia: Jessica Kingsley Publishers.

Fox. (n.d.). *Lie to me*. Retrieved March 7, 2011, from http://www.fox.com/lietome/about

Fox Searchlight Pictures (Producer), & Webb, M. (Director). (2009). *(500) Days of Summer* [Motion picture]. United States: Watermark, Sneak Preview Entertainment.

Frith, U. (2003). *Explaining the enigma* (2nd ed.). Oxford, United Kingdom: Blackwell.

Frith, U. (2004). Emanuel Miller lecture: Confusions and controversies about Asperger syndrome. *Journal of Child Psychology and Psychiatry, 45*(4), 672–686.

Frith, U. (2005). *If we knew what causes autism: Why it is important to talk about cognition*. Retrieved October 16, 2005, from http://www.awares.org/conferences

Frith, U., & Frith, C.D. (2006). The neural basis of mentalizing. *Neuron, 50*(4), 531–534.

Frith, C.D., & Wolpert, D. (Eds.). (2004). *The neuroscience of social interaction: Decoding, influencing, and imitating the actions of others*. New York: Oxford University Press.

Gallese, V. (2006). Intentional attunement: A neurophysiological perspective on social cognition and its disruption in autism. *Brain Research, 1079*, 15–24.

Garner, A. (1997). *Conversationally speaking: Tested new ways to increase your personal and social effectiveness* (3rd ed.). Los Angeles: Lowell House.

Gaston, L., & Marmar, C. (1994). The California Psychotherapy Alliance Scales. In A.O. Horvath & L.S. Greenberg (Eds.), *The working alliance: Theory, research, and practice* (pp. 85–108). New York: John Wiley & Sons.

Geller, L. (2009, Summer) Making inclusion work for students with Asperger Syndrome. *Autism Spectrum News, 1*, 32–42.

Gerhardt, P. (2000, Fall). Asperger Syndrome in adolescence and adulthood: Considerations for support and intervention [Electronic version]. *New Jersey Psychologist Magazine*.

Gerhardt, P. (2008, July). *Bridges to adulthood for learners with autism spectrum disorders: Targeting skills for the next environment*. Presented at Melmark Conference.

Gillberg, C. (2006). *The development of empathy*. Paper presented at The Social Brain 2 International Conference, Glasgow, Scotland.

Givens, D. (2011). *The nonverbal dictionary of gestures, signs and body language cues*. Retrieved July 9, 2010, from http://center-for-nonverbal-studies.org/6101.html

Global and Regional Asperger Syndrome Partnership & Organization for Autism Research. (n.d.). *The OAR/GRASP DVD/wmv guide for college professors*. Retrieved November 19, 2010, from http://www.grasp.org/new_art.htm

Golan, O., & Baron-Cohen, S. (2006). Systemizing empathy: Teaching adults with Asperger syndrome or high-functioning autism to recognize complex emotions using interactive multimedia. *Development and Psychopathology, 18*, 591-617.

Golan, O., Baron-Cohen, S., & Hill, J. (2006). The Cambridge Mindreading (CAM) Voice Battery: Testing emotional recognition in adults. *Journal of Autism and Developmental Disorders, 36*(2),169–183.

Goleman, D. (1995). *Emotional intelligence: Why it can matter more than IQ*. New York: Bantam Books.

Goleman, D. (1998). *Working with emotional intelligence*. New York: Random House.

Goleman, D. (2006). *Social intelligence*. New York: Random House.

Grandin, T. (n.d.). *Transition to employment and independent living for individuals with autism and Aspergers*. Retrieved February 24, 2010, from http://www.grandin.com/inc/transition.employment.autism.aspergers.html

Grandin, T. (1995). *Thinking in pictures and other reports from my life with autism.* New York: Vintage.

Grandin, T. (1999). *Choosing the right job for people with autism or Asperger syndrome.* Retrieved June 10, 2010, from http://www.aspennj.org/pdf/information/adult-issues/choosing-the-right-job-for-people-with-autism.pdf

Grandin, T., & Barron, S. (2005). *The unwritten rules of social relationships: Decoding social mysteries through the unique perspectives of autism.* Arlington, TX: Future Horizons.

Grandin, T., & Duffy, K. (2004). *Developing talents: Careers for individuals with Asperger syndrome and high-functioning autism.* Shawnee Mission, KS: Autism Asperger Publishing Company.

Gray, C. (2004, June). *Social stories for students with Asperger syndrome.* Autism Super Conference, Sacramento, CA.

Happé, F.G. (1994). An advanced test of theory of mind: Understanding of story characters' thoughts and feelings by able autistic, mentally handicapped, and normal children and adults. *Journal of Autism and Developmental Disorders, 24*(2), 129–154.

Happé, F.G. (2006). *Central coherence: Detail-focused cognitive style in ASD.* Presented at The Social Brain 2 International Conference, Glasgow, Scotland.

Hawkins, G. (2004). *How to find work that works for people with Asperger Syndrome.* Philadelphia: Jessica Kingsley Publishers.

Heimberg, R.G., & Becker, R.E. (2002). *Cognitive-behavioral group therapy for social phobia.* New York: Guilford Publishers.

Hénault, I. (2007). *Apserger's syndrome and sexuality: From adolescence through adulthood.* Philadelphia: Jessica Kingsley Publishers.

Hitchcock, A., & Bouzereau, L. (Producers), & Hitchcock, A., & Bouzereau, L. (Directors). (1954). *Dial M for murder* [Motion picture]. United States: Warner Brothers.

Holland, J.L. (1996). *Dictionary of Holland occupational codes.* Lutz, FL: Psychological Assessment Resources.

Holmes, H. (2008). *The well-dressed ape.* New York: Random House.

Horn, S. (1997). *What's holding you back?* New York: St Martin's Press.

Howlin, P. (2004). *Autism and Asperger syndrome: Preparing for adulthood* (2nd ed.). New York: Routledge.

Howlin, P., & Yates, P. (1999). The potential effectiveness of social skills groups for adults with autism. *Autism: International Journal of Research and Practice, 3,* 299–307.

Hughes, C., Cuth, C., Presley, J., Dye, M., & Byers, C. (2000). Teaching and learning in school: The Metropolitan Nashville Peer Buddy Program. In W.L. Heward *Exceptional children: An introduction to special education* (6th ed., pp. 526–527). Upper Saddle River, NJ: Merrill.

Iacoboni, M. (2009). *Mirroring people: The science of empathy and how we connect with others.* New York: Picador.

Individuals with Disabilities Education Improvement Act (IDEA) of 2004, PL 108-446, 20 U.S.C. §§ 1400 *et seq.*

Johnson, S. (2004). *Mind wide open: Your brain and the neuroscience of everyday life.* New York: Scribner.

Keltner, D. (2009). *Born to be good: The science of a meaningful life.* New York: WW Norton & Co.

Klin, A. (2000). Attributing social meaning to ambiguous visual stimuli in higher-functioning autism and Asperger's Syndrome, The Social Attribution Task. *Journal of Child Psychiatry and Psychology, 41*(7), 831–846.

Klin, A., Jones, W., Schultz, R., Volkmar, F., & Cohen, D. (2002). Defining and quantifying the social phenotype in autism. *Philosophical Transactions of the Royal Society Series B, 358,* 345–360.

Kluger, J. (2008, January 28). Why we love. *Time Magazine,* 55–60.

La Barre, W. (1947). The cultural basis of emotions and gestures. *Journal of Personality, 16,* 49–68.

Liddell, G.A., & Rasmussen, C. (2005). Memory profile of children with nonverbal learning disability. *Learning Disabilities Research and Practice, 20,* 137–141.

Luscombe, B. (2008, January 28). Why we flirt. *Time Magazine,* 62–65.

Mattick, R.P., & Clarke, J.C. (1998). Development and validation of measures of social phobia scrutiny fear and social interaction anxiety. *Behavior Research Therapy, 36*(4), 455–470.

McGee, G., Almeida, M., Sulzer-Azaroff, B., & Feldman, P. (1992). Promoting reciprocal interactions via peer incidental teaching. *Journal of Applied Behavior Analysis, 25,* 117–126.

McIntosh, D., Reichmann-Decker, A., Winkielman, P., & Wilbarger, J.L. (2006). *When the social mirror breaks: Deficits in automatic, but not voluntary, mimicry of emotional facial expression in autism.* Retrieved October 10, 2006, from http://www.awares.org/conferences

Meyer, R.N. (2001). *Asperger syndrome employment workbook: An employment workbook for adults with Asperger syndrome.* Philadelphia: Jessica Kingsley Publishers.

Minshew, N., & Williams, D. (2007). The new neurobiology of autism. *Archives of Neurology, 64*(7), 945–950.

Newline Cinema (Producer), & Cassavetes, N. (Director). (2004). *The notebook* [Motion picture]. United States: Gran Via, Avery Pix.

Newline Cinema (Producer), & Kwapis, K. (Director). (2009). *He's just not that into you* [Motion picture]. United States: Flower Films.

Newport, J. (2003). *Autism, sexuality and dating.* Plenary session presented at the annual meeting of the Autism Society of America, Pittsburgh.

Nylander, L., & Gillberg, C. (2001). Screening for autism spectrum disorders in adult psychiatric outpatients: a preliminary report. *ActaPsychiatrica Scandinavica, 103,* 428–434.

Oberman, L.M., & Ramachandran, V.S. (2007). Evidence for deficits in mirror neuron functioning, multisensory integration, and sound–form symbolism in autism spectrum disorders. *Psychological Bulletin, 133*(2), 310–327.

Oden, S., & Asher, S. (1977). Coaching children in social skills for friendship making. *Child Development, 48,* 495–506.

O'Donoghue, M. (Head writer) et al. (1977). Dating the self-conscious and extremely obnoxious [Skit in television series episode]. In *Saturday Night Live* (Season 3, Episode 8). New York: National Broadcasting Company.

Pease, B., & Pease, A. (2001). *Why men don't listen and women can't read maps: How we're different and what to do about it.* New York: Broadway Books.

Perner, L. (2002). *Preparing to be nerdy where nerdy can be cool: College planning for the high functioning student with autism.* Presented at the Autism Society of America, Indianapolis, IN.

Perry, N. (2008). *Adults on the autism spectrum leave the nest: Achieving supported independence.* Philadelphia: Jessica Kingsley Publishers.

Peterson, R. (2005). An examination of the relative effectiveness of training in nonverbal communication: Personal selling implications. *Journal of Marketing Education, 27*(2), 143–150.

Piven, J., Palmer, P., Jacobi, D., Childress, D., & Arndt, S. (1997). Broader autism phenotype: Evidence from a family history study of multiple-incidence autism families. *American Journal of Psychiatry, 154,* 185–190.

Premack, D., & Woodruff, G. (1978). Does the chimpanzee have a theory of mind? *Behavioral Brain Science, 1,* 515–526.

Prince-Hughes, D. (Ed.). (2002). *Aquamarine blue 5: Personal stories of college students with autism.* Athens: Ohio University Press.

Rafelson, B., & Wechsler, R. (Producers), & Rafelson, B. (Director). (1970). *Five easy pieces* [Motion picture]. United States: Sony Pictures.

Ramachandran, V.S. (2000). *Mirror neurons and imitation learning as the driving force behind "the great leap forward" in human evolution.* Retrieved July 9, 2010, from http://www.edge.org/3rd_culture/ramachandran/ramachandran_index.html.

Ramsay, R., Brodkin, E., Cohen, M., Ekman, E., Listerud, J., & Rostain, A. (2005). "Better strangers": Using the relationship in psychotherapy for adult patients with Asperger syndrome. *Psychotherapy: Theory, Research, Practice, Training, 42*(4), 483–493.

Ratey, J. (2001). *A user's guide to the brain.* New York: Random House.

Ratey, J., & Johnson, C. (1997). *Shadow syndromes: Recognizing and coping with the hidden psychological disorders that can influence your behavior and silently determine the course of your life.* New York: Random House.

Rizzolatti, G., Fadiga, L., Gallese, V., & Fogassi, L. (1996). Premotor cortex and the recognition of motor actions. *Brain Research, 3,* 131–141.

Robertson, S. (2008, March). *Transitioning to postsecondary education for students on the autism spectrum.* Plenary session presented at the Penn Autism Network Conference, Philadelphia.

Rourke, B.P. (1995). Identifying features of the syndrome of Nonverbal Learning Disabilities in children. *Perspectives: The Orton Dyslexia Society, 21,* 10–13.

Rostain, A., Cohen, M., & Brodkin, E. (2003). *Social Activities Scale.* Unpublished manuscript, University of Pennsylvania.

Schultz, R.T. (2005). Developmental deficits in social perception in autism: The role of the amygdala and fusiform face area. *International Journal of Developmental Neuroscience, 23,* 125–141.

Shore, S. (2001). *Beyond the wall: Personal experiences with autism and Asperger syndrome.* Shawnee Mission, KS: Autism Asperger Publishing Company.

Skirball, J.H. (Producer), & Hitchcock, A. (Director). (1943). *Shadow of a doubt* [Motion picture]. United States: Universal Studios.

Sperry, L.A., & Mesibov, G.B. (2005). Perceptions of social challenges of adults with autism spectrum disorder. *Autism, 9*(4), 362–376.

Stein, M., Goldin, P., Sareen, J., Zorilla, L., & Brown, G. (2002). Increased amygdala activation to angry and contemptuous faces in generalized anxiety disorder. *Archives of General Psychiatry, 59,* 1027–1034.

Stopa, L., & Clark, D.M. (2000). Social phobia and interpretation of social events. *Behaviour Research and Therapy, 38,* 273–283.

Tager-Flusberg, H. (2001). A re-examination of the theory of mind hypothesis of autism. In J. Burack & T. Charman, et al. (Eds.), *The development of autism: Perspectives from theory and research* (pp. 173–193). Mahwah, NJ: Lawrence Erlbaum Associates.

Tager-Flusberg, H. (2005). What neurodevelopmental disorders can reveal about cognitive architecture: the example of theory of mind. In *The structure of the innate mind* (pp. 3-24). New York: Oxford University Press.

Tantam, D. (2005). *What is there about Asperger Syndrome that is curable?* Retrieved October 15, 2005, from: http://www.awares.org/conferences

Theoret, H., Halligan, E., Kobayashi, M., Fregni, F., Tager-Flusberg, H., & Pascual-Leone, A. (2005). Impaired motor facilitation during action observation in individuals with autism spectrum disorder. *Current Biology, 15,* R84–R85.

TriStar Pictures (Producer), & Ephron, N. (Director). (1993). *Sleepless in Seattle* [Motion picture]. United States: TriStar Pictures.

Turner-Brown, L., Perry, T., Dichter, G., Bodfish, J., & Penn, D. (2008). Brief report: feasibility of social cognition and interaction training for adults with high functioning autism. *Journal of Autism and Developmental Disorders, 38,* 1777–1784.

University of California, Santa Barbara, Department of Sociology. (2009). *Basics of sexuality.* Retrieved from http://www.soc.ucsb.edu/sexinfo/category/basics-of-sexuality

Urdang, L., De Pencer, M., & Vanech, D. (Producers) & Mayer, M. (Director). (2009). *Adam* [Motion picture]. United States: Fox Searchlight Pictures.

U.S. Department of Labor. (2010). *Dictionary of occupational titles.* Retrieved January 6, 2010, from http://www.occupationalinfo.org

von Norman, A., Pilcher, L.D., Zaentz, P., Andrews, S.E., & Pollack, S. (Producers), & Minghella, A. (Director). (2000). *The talented Mr. Ripley* [Motion picture]. United States: Paramount Pictures.

Willey, L. (1999). *Pretending to be normal: Living with Asperger syndrome.* Philadelphia: Jessica Kingsley Publishers.

Willey, L. (2001). *Asperger syndrome in the family: Redefining normal.* Philadelphia: Jessica Kingsley Publishers.

Williams, D. (1998). *Somebody somewhere: Breaking free from the world of autism.* Philadelphia: Jessica Kingsley Publishers.

Zanuck, D.F. (Producer), & Mankiewicz, J.F. (Director). (1950). *All about Eve* [Motion picture]. United States: 20th-Century Fox.

Index

Page numbers followed by *t* indicate tables; page numbers followed by *f* indicate figures.